World Class

How to Lead, Learn and Grow like a Champion

Will Greenwood
and Ben Fennell

001

Ebury Edge, an imprint of Ebury Publishing,
20 Vauxhall Bridge Road,
London SW1V 2SA

Ebury Edge is part of the Penguin Random House group of companies
whose addresses can be found at global.penguinrandomhouse.com

First published in the United Kingdom by Ebury Edge in 2021

www.penguin.co.uk

A CIP catalogue record for this book is available from the British Library

ISBN 9780753558775

Printed and bound in Great Britain by Clays Ltd, Elcograf S.p.A.

The authorised representative in the EEA is Penguin Random House Ireland,
Morrison Chambers, 32 Nassau Street, Dublin D02 YH68.

Penguin Random House is committed to a sustainable
future for our business, our readers and our planet.
This book is made from Forest Stewardship Council®
certified paper.

This book is dedicated to every single person
out there who is trying to get better

Contents

Prologue   vii

Part I: Celebrating Difference

1. Selection   3
2. Feedback   23
3. Innovation   43
4. Decision-Making   61
5. Generosity   79

Part II: Forging Togetherness

6. Purpose   101
7. Coaching   119
8. Culture   137
9. Communication   159
10. Teamship   177

Part III: Accelerating Growth

11. Training   197
12. Pressure   215
13. Setbacks   235
14. Wellbeing   253
15. Speed   269

Conclusion   289
List of contributors   293
Acknowledgements   295
Index   299

Prologue

It was the wedding of the year – a royal wedding, no less – and I was at the evening reception in the grounds of Windsor Castle, a simple yet beautiful celebration of the marriage of Harry and Meghan. OK, so I fluffed my opening line to George Clooney when I was standing next to him at the urinal – you don't get a second chance at that, trust me – but when two lads from opposite sides of the Pennines hit the dance floor, it was as if nothing else mattered.

Greenwood and Tindall were at it again – Old Big Nose and Old Bent Nose were busting some moves like no one was watching. We often joked that the lad from Wakefield, Mike Tindall, was at one point sixteenth in line to the throne. He's much further back in the peloton now that Will and Kate have three children, but I was still impressed. More impressed than our audience on the dance floor seemed to be, anyway.

It wasn't our first dance-off. The most memorable one had been in Cargo Bar in Sydney, in the early hours of 23 November 2003, just after we'd won the Rugby World Cup: the same two buffoons and many of the same moves, just a different location and guest list. Although we did have *cricketing* royalty with us in Cargo that night: I spent a couple of hours talking to Brett Lee and Damien Martyn about cricket, in what was one of the most memorable sporting conversations I've ever had.

It felt good to be going at it again, bringing our unique interpretation of modern dance to a crowded dance floor. Tindall dances better than me. He can properly move; I just *think* I can. And that's just one way in which Mike and I are different, both physically and mentally.

When I say he couldn't pass and I couldn't tackle, I'm only half exaggerating. Mike was strong and I wasn't. I could pass with variety and flow; he couldn't. I could unlock a defence; he could blast through it. I could see a space very early; he could turn a small gap into a big one.

Tindall is relaxed to the point of being horizontal, while I often feared my own shadow. I knew every single play for the forwards and the backs; he only knew the ones that involved him. I knew where the ball would be in five phases' time; he didn't know where it was unless he had it in his hands. But none of this mattered because my weaknesses were his strengths, and vice versa. Over time, we learned that our complementary differences as individuals were our greatest strengths as a partnership. We could each do things that the other couldn't.

We amplified each other's strengths and covered for each other's weaknesses. I rarely let him pass; he rarely made me tackle. I was a space-hunter, looking for and identifying opportunities to attack, multiple phases in advance; Mike was a space-filler, knocking lumps out of people with or without the ball. I was a piano player; he was a piano shifter. I was an architect; he was a wrecking ball. We were both individually flawed, but together we conquered the world.

As we stood in the tunnel in Sydney, seconds before the biggest game of our lives, our mindsets were very different. I was feeling the pressure, soaked in self-doubt, and the silence was deafening. I looked to my left to see Tindall stride across the tunnel and slap Stirling Mortlock on the backside: 'Yeah, baby,' he said. 'This is why we play.' It was as if he was about to run out for a game of touch rugby with some mates.

Training was a constant reminder of our differences. I liked to nail down every scenario, to plan for the worst and to role play 'what-if' scenarios, with and without the ball. Mike never worried about any of that, not least because he knew that I was worrying for both of us. He never cut corners, but he worked differently to me, with less structure and routine. We wanted the same things, but we prepared for games very differently. I wanted freedom within a framework, while he wanted to kick the framework down the hallway.

Brutal honesty about our capabilities was the foundation upon which our partnership was built. We had no shame in articulating our strengths and weaknesses. It didn't mean we didn't put effort into our 'work-ons' – the things we could improve – but we both knew that we couldn't be world class at everything.

With this level of honesty, our trust and confidence grew – both in ourselves and in each other. Over time, our differences became a multiplier for our growing partnership. What we couldn't do individually didn't matter, because we hunted as a pair. Always different, but always together.

This book is an exploration of world-class performance and, quite fittingly, it is the product of another partnership. While it has been written in my voice, don't be fooled: it is the product of another partnership of different skills and complementary perspectives. While I played international rugby for eight years and was part of the World Cup-winning England team in 2003, my writing partner Ben Fennell has 16 years' CEO experience at Bartle Bogle Hegarty (BBH), one of the world's top advertising agencies. Ben ran BBH's business in Asia Pacific and the UK, leading a team that delivered exponential revenue and profit growth. During his time at BBH, he helped some of the world's biggest businesses and brands to grow, including Unilever, Diageo, British Airways, Virgin Media and Tesco. The growth that Ben and his team helped deliver was powered by exceptionally high levels of staff pride and colleague engagement, and on his watch, BBH spent ten consecutive years in the *Sunday Times* 100 Best Companies to Work For list. Ben set up The Growth House in 2018 with a singular purpose: to help leaders, teams and businesses grow. His company now works with many of the UK's biggest businesses, helping them to build winning teams and establish high-performance behaviours.

The simple ambition to be better has been the driving force throughout our two very different lives, and it's been central to our 30-year-long friendship. We met at Durham University in 1991, were best man at one another's weddings, and have challenged, coached and encouraged each other ever since.

We didn't want to simply write a sports book or a business book – we wanted to write a book about sport *and* business. We wanted to take the most insightful learnings from both worlds and present them with one specific goal in mind: to help people become better. We will build the case that personal growth is the first step towards all the other kinds of growth in business: revenue growth, profit growth and increased shareholder value. We want leaders to create a virtuous circle where their personal growth powers the growth of the collective. To that end, we have mined our contacts from the cream of the sporting and business worlds, as well as calling upon our experiences with the leaders who have inspired and challenged us. We want to provide insights and inspiration, and to share tools and techniques that will help you to grow.

Throughout the writing of this book, while speaking to leaders and top performers in business and sport, one idea revealed itself to us again and again. It came to sit above all the others, and it runs through this book like words through a stick of rock. It's the idea that if you celebrate difference and forge togetherness, you will accelerate growth.

Not all the leaders we spoke to used those exact words, but they always described these concepts. They are at the heart of all of the strongest cultures we have looked at, and they constitute the winning formula that makes up our belief system, our growth strategy and the three sections of this book:

Difference multiplied by **Togetherness** delivers **Growth**

In the book's first part, we will explore the importance of **selecting** for difference. One important caveat is that this is not a book about race or gender – there are people with far more expertise than Ben and I on the topics of diversity, inclusion and belonging. It remains an uncomfortable truth that while talent is distributed evenly across society, opportunity is not. While we wholeheartedly support the mission to create more diverse leadership cohorts in every business, we have chosen to make *cognitive* diversity our focus.

Through this lens we will explore challenge and **feedback**, showing that elite teams are not scared of disagreement but just know how to disagree effectively. We will look at the importance of **generosity** and examine the value of different perspectives, skills and stimuli in **decision-making** and **innovation**.

In the second part of the book, we will argue that the first step in forging **togetherness** is developing a strong and meaningful **purpose**, a North Star to guide your team. We will explore the importance of **culture**, and how it is slowly built but easily damaged. **Communication** is at the heart of togetherness, and we will analyse the written, verbal and non-verbal language that the best leaders deploy to bring their people together. We will explore the value of world-class **coaching** and the often undervalued role of **teamship**, noting that many executives are so focused on developing their leadership that they neglect the skills and behaviours required to be a great teammate.

In the final part of the book, we will explore **growth**, starting with **training** and the importance of fostering a learning environment so that you can strive to get better, both individually and collectively. We will address **pressure**, before looking at **well-being**. We will learn how resilience is built by **setbacks** and share how the best in sport and business use these painful moments to fuel future success. And finally, we will look at the game-changer that is **speed**, a quality that can devastate your competition.

There is no single chapter on leadership, because it is a key element in every chapter. We will argue that harnessing difference and togetherness to create growth is the most fundamental aspect of modern leadership. Every organisation needs to manage this tension and find an optimal balance. With too much difference and not enough togetherness, you will have a collection of individuals. With too much togetherness and not enough difference, you will only get one view of the mountain. In every team and in every partnership, the magic is in the blend. You want diverse skills but a shared vision, one culture but a multiplicity of leadership archetypes.

Everywhere that we found excellence and growth, we also found difference and togetherness. It is a truth that revealed itself to us at every turn, and one that we want to share with you. Irrespective of your occupation or sporting pedigree, whether you're leading one person or 1,000, we want this book to help you grow. We want to help you to build teams that are more dynamic, more effective and more generous. Teams that know how to win, but also how to deal with setbacks and loss. Teams that know how to challenge and support each other. Teams that are brave and kind. Teams that celebrate difference and forge togetherness.

PART I

Celebrating
Difference

1. Selection

'A mix of very different people will not only get
you to your destination faster, they will make
the journey a whole lot more interesting.'

DIFFERENCE | TOGETHERNESS | GROWTH

Sir Clive Woodward delivers a brilliant after-dinner anecdote about what it felt like to address his England squad. Up at the front, within arm's length, would be senior players like the captain Martin Johnson, Lawrence Dallaglio and Jason Leonard. They were the Godfathers, and Woodward would often wait for them to nod their approval before proceeding. Then came the Students, the guys scribbling away furiously in their notebooks: Jonny Wilkinson, Neil Back, Richard Hill, all analysts of the game, ready to take anything apart and scrutinise it. Next came the Outside Backs, and you could never be sure if they were truly present: Ben Cohen, Dan Luger, Iain Balshaw. Keeping them focused was tough. Then, finally, came the Scrum Halves, small in stature but all massive personalities: Matt Dawson, Austin Healey, Andy Gomarsall, frantically trying to chip in with a wise crack. 'Try coaching that crowd,' Clive says with a smile.

We might all have looked pretty similar, but looks can be deceptive. Like the Avengers, we each had our own superpower, but with that power came plenty of challenges and challengers. Clive was a strong enough leader to know that he needed big characters in his side, and he also needed complementary difference. We had extroverts and introverts, graduates and tradesmen, inexperienced internationals and British and Irish Lions.

This exploration of celebrating difference begins with selection, which is to a leader what choosing ingredients is to a chef. Clive has often said that selection is 50 per cent of coaching.

Your strategy and tactics can be flawless, your training can be world class, but if you haven't got the right people in the right positions, you are going to make things very hard for yourself.

In business, recruitment is every bit as important as selection is in sport. Before you go anywhere, you need to make sure that you've got the right people on the bus. A mix of different people will not only get you to your destination faster, they will make the journey a whole lot more interesting.

A leader usually inherits a team at the start of their tenure – the team assembled by their predecessor. A good leader will ask themselves: is there enough difference in this team? Can these individuals challenge and collaborate effectively? And most importantly, do the skills and capabilities match the ambition of the mission? It's critical to understand that the team that has got you to where you *are* may not be the one that will get you where you want to go. And it is vital not to see selection as a task only for the early stages of a team's formation. The best leaders are always reviewing the composition and performance of their team, and assessing how well suited each individual is to the ever-changing environment they find themselves in. Dana Strong, who at the time of writing is president of consumer services for Comcast, makes an interesting point about when and how to change a team: 'Don't pick your team too fast. Make sure that you really understand what you have, and really sit with it. Some mistakes I've made were making too many changes too quickly,' she says.

So when it comes to packing your team with difference, what can business learn from sport?

RECRUIT FOR DIFFERENCE

Say the word 'diversity' in a business context and the discussion will inevitably turn to subjects like gender, race and disability. And that is absolutely as it should be – many companies are still falling a long way short in these areas. The point that you have to 'see it to be it' is made powerfully with regard to all forms of diversity. It is very hard to forge a connection or envision a long-term career in a company that has nobody around the top table who looks or sounds like you. You want employees to look up and see consistent quality coupled with an abundance of difference.

Diversity of gender, race and upbringing are all critical drivers of cognitive difference. We are all a product of our upbringing and life experience, and it's hard to separate who we are and what we think from where we've come from. Our world view is coloured by the people we have been surrounded by and the experiences that have shaped us. If you truly want to celebrate difference, you need to build a team that is diverse in the way it looks, sounds and thinks.

Put simply, a team that is cognitively diverse will include people who solve problems in very different ways. There should be strategic thinkers, creative thinkers and operational thinkers. People who see opportunity and those who identify problems; people who are intuitive and those who are more data led. Recruiting for difference should be at the forefront of any leader's mind as they begin their selection process.

This is a lesson that has been absorbed by the elite units in the military. Jason Fox was a special forces soldier for over 20 years. You might know him as 'Foxy' from the television series *SAS: Who Dares Wins*. Jason knows a great deal about the composition of elite teams and the power of diversity to enhance operational excellence. 'It's a weakness of a team if you're all coming at things from the same angle,' he says. 'You want difference and you want challenge. You need headstrong people to drive the team forward, but you also need compassionate people to rein those headstrong people in. You need creative people who can think outside the box and not get freaked out when the plan doesn't go to plan. You need thinkers who are stubborn, driven, creative, flexible and compassionate. You also need some really precise guys who are sticklers for detail. That's what an SAS team will look like. It's a blend of all those different types of person.'

Andy Fennell (no relation to Ben) was the global chief marketing officer of Diageo, one of the world's biggest producers of beer and spirits, with brands including Smirnoff, Johnnie Walker and Guinness. He talks about the diversity that existed in the finest team he ever led: 'There was a good gender balance and we had leaders from half a dozen different countries, but it was the cognitive difference that made this team special. One was obsessed with ideas, another with rigour. One asserted standards constantly, however unpopular it made him, and one brought flair and harmony. One wanted to disrupt everything, another wanted to just get on with things. We checked our alignment to our purpose and principles regularly, but my main job as the leader was to encourage each of them to play their natural game.'

We're naturally drawn to people who are like us, and a common pitfall is for leaders to recruit in their own image – often subconsciously. But a team or partnership that is too similar will never be as powerful as one that contrasts and complements. It takes a confident leader to pack their team with difference. Abraham Lincoln famously created a 'Team of Rivals' when he included three of his competitors for the Republican Party nomination in his Cabinet, knowing that it was only by creating tension within his top team that he could fully interrogate his ideas and torture-test his thinking.

Dave Lewis led a remarkable turnaround during his six years as CEO of Tesco, the UK's biggest retailer. He inherited a business that had lost its way, following an accounting scandal that had shaken the business to its core, with colleague engagement low and supplier relationships fraught. When his time at the retailer finished, he left behind a business with 16 quarters of consecutive growth. He describes how he embraced cognitive difference to shape his strategy for the business:

'I have a group of four or five people who I go to when I start a new job. The key point is that they are all so completely different to me. I'll share some thinking with them and we will disagree on about 90 per cent of what I've shared, but each one of them will give me a perspective that I would never have got to on my own.'

Having your thinking challenged is always a good thing, because one of three things will happen:

1. Your arguments will hold up well under interrogation and your commitment to them will sharpen and strengthen.
2. Your arguments will evolve and they will be built upon by the challenge.
3. The flaws in your arguments will be exposed at an early stage and you will develop better ones as a consequence.

A confident leader understands when to hold firm and when to give ground. They use the difference they have baked into their top team to interrogate a strategy with vigour, so that when it's time to go public, they know that it's robust.

Rich Pierson is the CEO and co-founder of Headspace, a company famous for making meditation and mindfulness more mainstream and accessible. At the time of writing, the Headspace app has had more than 6 million downloads, with 2.5 million paying subscribers in 190 countries. 'Our team is a mash-up of very different skills and backgrounds,' he says. 'We have a former Buddhist monk, a team of behavioural scientists, content creators from Disney, product managers from Amazon and creatives from advertising, plus enterprise and sales people. Managing that difference, embracing that tension, is the hardest thing to get right, but it's always where the magic happens.'

In business, a good team is not one that doesn't disagree; it's one that knows *how* to disagree. Team members will challenge ideas with rigour, but also with respect and emotional intelligence. They will know that there's a difference between the challenge that's required privately and the alignment that's required publicly. We've all received feedback that felt personal and unhelpful, lacking context or delivered in a way that felt undermining. The opposite might also be true – feedback that felt generous and task-focused, that was intended to make the team and the mission better. Ben spends a lot of time coaching the skills within teams to challenge and disagree respectfully. They need to be learned and they need to be practised – like a muscle in the body, these skills will fade and diminish if they are not worked regularly.

'Agree, disagree, commit,' Rich says. 'It's the job of the leader to ensure that enough discussion happens where leaders can agree and disagree. However, once the decision has been made, everyone has to act like the decision was theirs. There can be no gaps between your teammates. One leader who does not share the values, despite having great skills, can put the whole culture at risk.'

THE MAGIC IS IN THE BLEND

To get a seat at Sir Clive Woodward's top table as a coach, you needed to bring expertise and difference. He recruited a team of coaches with different perspectives but shared values. He was a visionary and a motivator, but he was also a good delegator. He shared control and authority and he empowered his coaches. His coach selection, much like his player selection, was a masterclass in difference.

Phil Larder was our defence coach. He came from rugby league and focused on drills, detail, repetition and accountability. He barked out orders, scaring you out of your skin, like a perma-tanned Action Man in shorts. Contrast that with Brian Ashton, our attack coach, who was a smiler, a whisperer and would coax you out of your skin. Our coaching sessions would combine seemingly contradictory messages, like 'relentless consistency in defence' from Phil and 'play what you see and hunt the space in attack' from Brian. We had a Roundhead in Phil, laying down a framework, and a Cavalier in Brian, preaching freedom. While a good player can hold both thoughts in his head at the same time, the differing approaches of the coaches naturally appealed to different players in the group.

Different leaders will connect with different people, which is why having a range of archetypes in your leadership or coaching group is so important. You want people to look at the top of the organisation and see a whole spectrum of different styles and personalities, not least so that they can imagine themselves there. Philip Jansen, CEO of BT, says, 'In the teams I build, I want technical expertise and I want people who are new to the category. I want optimists and pessimists. As ever, it's all about creating balance.'

Ben runs a powerful programme for clients, in which he invites eight to ten inspirational speakers, with different backgrounds and super-strengths, to talk about leadership and teamship. The skill in putting the list together is curating a truly diverse set of archetypes, but inviting them to talk about a consistent set of topics. If enough difference is baked into the list of speakers, two things start to happen: firstly, consistent themes emerge, but they are expressed in a relentlessly fresh and different way. Secondly, people start to look back at themselves and think: 'I can be successful by being my own kind of leader, with my own leadership style.' Win-win.

Jeff Dodds is the chief operating officer of Virgin Media, a £5 billion business. He makes the straightforward point that diversity in your business will help you to better represent and understand your range of customers: 'Creating greater diversity is not only the right thing to do, it's also the most effective thing to do, because it creates the most accelerated growth for your business. Our customer base is half the country, so if we want to really understand our customers, we need to reflect and represent them. Your leadership group needs to have diversity in all forms, the same amount of difference that is found in society.'

PEOPLE WHO KNOW ALL THE RULES
AND PEOPLE WHO DON'T

A less explored driver of difference within a team is the mixture of youth and experience. The Great Britain women's hockey team for the 2016 Rio Olympic Games in 2016 was composed of both the 'old guard' of Kate and Helen Richardson-Walsh and Alex Danson, with over a thousand caps between them, and the youthful exuberance of Lily Owsley, Joie Leigh and Shona McCallin. They won the gold medal.

If you look closely at the data regarding Rugby World Cup-winning teams, the total number of caps or even average caps can be misleading; it's the blend that matters most. The players with a handful of caps can be just as crucial as those with a hundred. Think of the England forwards Sam Underhill and Tom Curry at the 2019 World Cup, relative newbies to the international game. They went into the tournament having played a few games for England between them and both completely over-delivered. England were the youngest team to take part in a World Cup final, and while they might not have won it, they pulled off one of the greatest efforts from an England team in living history in beating the All Blacks in the semi-final.

A blend of youth and experience is mutually beneficial, fostering an environment in which the young learn from the old and the old are energised by the young. Nick Gill was Ben's long-time creative partner at BBH and is one of the great advertising and creative gurus of his generation – think Levi's, Lynx and the Surf bubble man. He talks about the fact that BBH's best work was often created when there was a blend of 'old masters and Young Turks – people who know all the rules, and people who know none of them.'

I've always felt that a human being is at their most effective at the point in their life when experience and energy converge. As a business leader, there might be a ten-year window – it is shorter for an athlete – when you are in your absolute prime. Before that, you have the energy but lack the experience; after, you might have the experience but the batteries will be starting to run a little low. The same is true in a team. You want to blend the enthusiasm and optimism of individuals who are new to the top table with those who have the muscle memory and the scars of battle.

DIFFERENCE UNITED

THE HOLY TRINITY

In our World Cup-winning team, nobody was individually perfect, but we all complemented and covered for each other. I've already described my partnership with Mike Tindall, but there were other combinations in our team that were equally complementary. Think of 'the Holy Trinity' of Richard Hill, Neil Back and Lawrence Dallaglio, our much-celebrated back row. Neil Back was the chop tackler, the uber-fit link man. Richard Hill was like Mr White from *Reservoir Dogs*, patrolling, cleaning, tidying and fixing. And Dallaglio was Thor from the Avengers, the huge character with the big plays, the big runs and the big jaw. Nobody was perfect; together they were absolutely world class. They acknowledged their work-ons – Backy worked on his hands, Hilly on his lineout and Lawrence on his tackle technique, and it was fascinating to see what good coaches they were to each other – but they didn't obsess about them. They were much more focused on their strengths.

Early in the life cycle of an executive team, it is worth taking the time to share the strengths and work-ons of the group. Work-ons aren't weaknesses – that's a passive label that suggests they are beyond our control; repositioning them as work-ons is much more active. You might never be world class at a work-on, but you can certainly improve. Not only is it empowering for people to understand that they don't have to be top of their field at everything, but it's also inspiring when complementary partnerships emerge. If Bob is strategic and Barbara is operational, then they'll have each other covered. Sally doesn't have to be great at numbers, because David is. These kind of partnerships can lead to powerful peer-on-peer coaching and support. You might open topics up while your partner might close them down, and that creates a powerful combination.

'When I evaluate talent, I use a simple triangle: strategic thinking, networking and operational delivery,' says Jeff Dodds of Virgin Media. 'Everyone in the team tends to score differently against those three criteria. And of course, there will be an overall team score. You want a team with very high scores across different criteria. I'll look at my team sometimes and observe that we have become light on one of those areas and I'll need to invest or upweight one of the capabilities. I observe that elite performers often tend to have big super-strengths and big weaknesses.'

The challenge for the leader is to get their senior team to raise their heads from their own specialist areas and point their expertise at the broader agenda of the business. A group of people who never get out of their own 'swim lane' and interrogate a challenge together is not really a team; they are a collection of experts. A great team harvests the collective wisdom of the group to problem-solve. They are expert, but not parochial. They know when to stay in their lanes and when not to. And it's important that the leader signals how and when they want this to happen.

A smart leader will have the self-awareness to know where their strengths lie and what they need around them to perform at their best. This is doubly true for a business founder, who will also have to understand that the leadership behaviours and capabilities required in the 'start-up' phase will often evolve as they move into the 'scale-up' phase.

Sarah Willingham is an entrepreneur and investor who specialises in the restaurant trade, and is known for her past role as a dragon on the TV show *Dragons' Den*. I asked her about the leadership challenges that growth can pose for founders. 'Anyone who's any good in the restaurant business can grow their first restaurant to a group of four or five,' she says. 'By the time you get to that size, however, things will start to get really stretched. The founders will often need to bring in new people at this stage, people who have experience of operating at that kind of scale and above. Unless, of course, you are one of those unicorns who can shift gears and evolve your leadership skills for the next phase of growth.'

Rich Pierson from Headspace may well be one of those unicorns. He sums up the challenge nicely: 'You need different kinds of people

to take the business to the next stage. For the company to be dura-
ble, you need people who can do things that the founders can't.'

Starting and scaling a business are quite different tasks that
require quite different skills and behaviours. Having the confidence to hire for what you need in the future rather than what has
served you in the past is a particularly valuable strength in a leader.

SELECT FOR YOUR STYLE OF PLAY

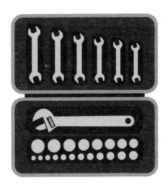

You need players who will deliver on your mission and suit
your style and culture. The best all-round player might not
always get recruited if he or she doesn't suit your framework.
Good leaders know that selection will differ according to the
task, the competition or the context. The England rugby head
coach Eddie Jones is very good at making the point that selection
is always bespoke and focused on both the short- and longer-term
strategy. The selection of Tom Curry at number eight in 2020
mystified many. He might not have been the best number eight in
England, but Eddie wanted him playing there because it suited
his plans for Tom's development. Eddie says that he regrets not
changing his selection after the brilliant World Cup semi-final
win against New Zealand. He broke his golden rule and kept the

same team in place for the final, rather than acknowledging that South Africa posed a very different threat.

Selection is equally strategic in business; you have to recruit for difference. Here's Andy Fennell again:

'As the bar and club landscape began to evolve, we changed the recruitment brief for sales people in Diageo. We used a simple criterion and personality descriptor at interview: "We are looking for the kind of people who can get into nightclubs without paying."'

Diageo wanted to find gregarious people with confidence and emotional intelligence, people who would get on well with bar owners – their CV was less important than their personality.

'That change transformed our sales capability,' continues Andy. 'We went from having a highly educated, highly strategic group of analytical sales people, to people who were much more credible with the owners of the bars we were trying to sell to.' It's a great example of how a shift in selection according to your style of play can power your growth.

DIFFERENCE DRIVES PERFORMANCE

With the right selection in place, that magic blend of educational background, personality type, race, gender, age and thinking, we can move into the next phase of the journey: binding the team together with a shared vision, a shared purpose and a shared code of conduct. These should not just be words in a PowerPoint presentation, but a genuine commitment to a few binding principles and ideas.

This is the task that faces every British and Irish Lions team in its first few weeks. Leaders such as Sir Ian McGeechan, the legendary Lions player and coach, are masters at taking a group of individuals from four separate nations and bringing them together in a pre-tour camp. In the early days of building the team, individuals are invited to share their back stories, to talk about the things that matter to them most and where they've come from. The coaches will be trying to not only bring the group together, but also to establish the tour's code of conduct and style of play. On a gruelling six weeks in the southern hemisphere, you don't just need great players – you need great characters, too.

Businesses use their purpose and their values to help them select as well as lead. Here's Rich Pierson from Headspace again: 'At the heart of everything we do is our member promise: "To inspire, guide and support our members to create healthy and happy routines that last a lifetime." All of our leadership training flows from that core promise. It has been iterated and refined over time, but the sentiment has been there from the start. It brings together an internal and an external message that is relevant for our members and the members of our team.'

Difference, coupled with a strong sense of purpose, has the power to drive performance and offers you the best chance to respond to challenges rapidly and more imaginatively. In times of crisis, it can be what separates a business that thrives from one that struggles to keep its head above water.

When we spoke to Dave Lewis of Tesco for this book, ten weeks into the Covid-19 lockdown in 2020, he was humbled by the performance he was witnessing from his staff: 'The applied expertise and creativity that has come to the fore during this time of crisis has been incredible. It's been inspiring to watch how different people with different skills have come together to solve problems. They changed every rule. Pre-crisis, our plan was to double our online capacity in three years; during the crisis, we doubled the online business in four weeks. We went from 600,000 deliveries per week to 1.3 million. That's like building two and a half Ocados. It's been epic.'

Under the most extreme pressure, a team with very different skills but a shared mission helped to feed the nation. If you ever wanted to quantify the power of a diverse team, there it is.

World-Class Selection: Highlights

1. Embracing difference should come in many forms: gender, race and cognitive diversity, to name just three. You need creative thinkers, strategic thinkers and organisational thinkers, so pack your team with difference.

2. A good team isn't one that doesn't disagree; it's one that knows *how* to disagree.

3. Resist the impulse to recruit in your own image. After all, a team of similar archetypes only has one view of the mountain.

4. See it to be it: different leaders connect with different people. Educational background, personality type, age, gender, race – people want to see that people like them have made it to the top.

5. A good team should be representative of the customers it is trying to serve.

6. Youth or experience? You need a good mixture of both – people who know all the rules and people who know none of them.

7. Real difference, united by a shared purpose, will give you the best chance of winning.

2. Feedback

'Delivering feedback is always a balancing act; it should be challenging but kind, it should address work-ons but build on strengths, it should be high-cadence but not overwhelming.'

DIFFERENCE   TOGETHERNESS   GROWTH

'Rugby is not for you, Greenwood.' These were the damning words of my England under-18 report at the end of a two-week summer training camp in 1990. The coaches had tested our athletic prowess, skills and decision-making with the best of our age group from all four corners of the country.

I was a late developer. Even though I'm an October birthday, my hormones just did not kick in until I was nearly 20. I still wasn't shaving, I had a high-pitched voice, there was no chance of me being served in any pub except my local and nightclubs were a definite no-go zone. We know about the advantages of having a birthday close to the start of the academic year; I seemed to have missed out on all of them.

So when I trained with the best of the best as a 17-year-old, I found the physical stuff a monumental struggle. It was terrifying, and I had to survive on my skills and my wits. Only later in life would I hear a quote from *The Rule of Four* by Ian Caldwell and Dustin Thomason, a line that might have been written for me: 'The strong take from the weak, but the smart take from the strong.'

At England under-18s, those who could not cope physically found it tough to get a game, and that meant me. My report gave me reasonable scores for endurance running – I weighed about 60 kilograms, so that was never a problem – but my lanky frame struggled when the contact element came in. The coaches knew I could play cricket – I was county standard at the time – so I was told in no uncertain terms, in black and white: 'Greenwood should consider pursuing other sports.' When your father had played, captained and coached England at rugby, it was a bitter pill to swallow. That report has stayed with me ever since – it hurt then and it still hurts now.

There was no context, no framing and no light at the end of the tunnel. I never played for England at schoolboy level, which was a big knockback. I can see now, however, that how I was treated then gave me the hunger and desire to make myself better, to prove people wrong and to create accelerated learning and growth for myself.

I've now been away from the pitch for 15 years. I've worked with many world-class companies and I've studied some truly elite outfits, such as the Royal Marines and the SAS. They are all different, but they have one thing in common: they all know how to give and receive high-quality feedback. So how do they do it?

FEEDBACK REQUIRES CONTEXT

C🌍NTEXT

The further I get from my playing days, the more I believe that the culture that Sir Clive Woodward and our team created was unique and special. The second point of our team code of conduct, signed off by all the players, read as follows:

'We are encouraged to discuss openly and honestly in the War Room all aspects of training/playing – we are working in a no 'if only' culture. If we think there is a problem with any areas of the programme, then this must be discussed in confidence in the War Room with the appropriate people.'

Clive wanted feedback in every direction: coach to player, coach to coach, player to player and player to coach. Giving everyone the opportunity to talk was empowering, and within the context of our no 'if only' culture, it meant that the feedback was geared towards a single goal: improving the quality of the training, coaching and organisation, and consequently improving the team. When someone spoke up, we listened and received the feedback in the spirit in which it was intended. We didn't shoot the messenger; we embraced him. Our team code had set the context: we lived and policed it.

Feedback without context can feel like criticism, but if you've played sport as a youngster or grown up being coached, receiving feedback in the workplace will feel more familiar. I know that Ben was struck when he started at BBH that not everyone felt the same way about feedback as he did. He saw it as a critical part of the learning process. Having played rugby for England Colts and England Students under-21s, he was not only comfortable with feedback but craved it. In contrast, he watched his fellow graduate trainees view feedback as criticism and observed how it knocked their confidence. Ben realised there and then that his background in sport had given him a huge head start: he had learned how to learn.

The experience taught him that it was always worth taking the time to explain his approach to feedback to the increasingly large teams that he led. He never again presumed that everyone viewed feedback in the same way that he did. He made it a 'terms of engagement' conversation with every new team member to present the context around his approach.

The first step in delivering effective feedback is ensuring that the recipient understands that your feedback is only intended to make them improve. Before focusing on 'what', it pays to spend a moment on 'why'. The why should always connect the feedback to the growth of the recipient. A narrative that Ben would often use with anyone who wanted to progress went as follows: 'If I can help you to grow, then this team will grow, and so will our business. If you are willing to listen and to learn, if you are willing to put away any defensiveness and treat feedback as a gift, then I will be really generous. I will give you feedback all the time, and over time your growth will accelerate, and so will your career.'

It's hard to give feedback to an individual you don't know very well, and who doesn't know you. High-performing teams will take the time to create that knowledge and context so that difficult conversations become much more manageable. Emily Scarratt, who is a World Cup winner, World Rugby's 2019 women's player of the year and England's record Six Nations point-scorer, says: 'In a team sport like ours, it's really important to understand each other as people; if you understand the person, you will understand the athlete. We would take the time to understand each individual's expectations, values and beliefs. If you create an environment of mutual trust and respect, then you will be able to have tough conversations and show vulnerability, knowing that it's all for the greater good.'

This narrative creates an unwritten contract, a framework within which feedback is contextualised and understood.

BE CHALLENGING, BUT BE KIND

Even the toughest feedback can be given with generosity and emotional intelligence. Ben's successor at BBH, the CEO Karen Martin, has a wonderful mantra: 'Be tough on the issue but soft on the person.' If you can direct your feedback at the issue rather than the individual, there's a much better chance it will land. When someone feels attacked, their defences go up. They start to defend their position or behaviour rather than really listening to the feedback.

Many of us have someone in our lives who has the ability to cut to the heart of an issue and deliver the kind of honesty that the toughest situations require. Ben and I have always played this role for each other. These people are invaluable, especially as you progress to more senior positions in your work. They tend to be comfortable in their own skin and unafraid of speaking truth to power. Once you find this kind of *consigliere*, you should keep them close. They will challenge you without agenda. They will tell you what you *need* to hear, rather than what you might *want* to hear. Often, they will amplify the nagging concern that has been a whisper in your head. The confident and mature leader will not only make themselves open to this kind of challenge, but will actively seek it out.

For every one of the England and Lions games I played in, my dad gave me written feedback in the form of a touch-by-touch breakdown of my performance. My best effort, in his eyes, was for the midweek Lions in South Africa in 1997, against the Free State Cheetahs, the unofficial fourth Test. My performance was still nowhere near perfect, of course, and the reasons why were laid bare in front of me. After one game against Australia towards the end of my career, I received the following bit of fatherly feedback: 'Two carries in the game; does this represent lack of opportunity or lack of ambition?' My old man is shrewd. He could sense my loss of confidence and knew I needed to reboot if I was to make the Lions tour in 2005. Feedback delivered as a question is golden, because it means that the individual has to find the answer themselves.

When it comes to feedback, your tone really matters. I've witnessed coaches get it horribly wrong, and the impact can be devastating, especially to a young person. So much of sport and life is about confidence, and you can really damage it with clumsy or badly delivered feedback.

Many elite rowers have a principle around delivering feedback immediately and in the moment. They call it 'on the riverbank', which means that the first thing you do once you get out of the water is debrief the session and cover any issues. Whether it lasts two minutes or much longer, what matters is that it becomes a habit, the final part of the session.

In the special forces, there is a strict debriefing process. Special forces veteran Jason Fox explains: 'Feedback and learning is baked into the after-action review process in the special forces. After an immediate and then a more considered review, the learnings are written up and shared. Here's the really interesting bit: those learnings from the battlefield are sent immediately to the people leading training back at base camp. This means that training is always relevant and always up to date. The feedback loop is closed, as the very latest experiences and learning are fed immediately into the latest training programmes.'

This is a culture that has baked feedback into its process. The best management consultancies, the likes of McKinsey and Bain, have a similar approach. Over many years, they have instilled the idea that the project is not completed until the case study and key learnings are written up and circulated. When a process like this becomes an unconscious competency, it becomes a habit.

At a senior level in an organisation, the ability to give and receive feedback is critical. When it is done well, teammates are constructive, challenging and generous. But when it is done badly, the energy is completely different. In the corporate world, there can be point-scoring, cheap shots and even apathy. A good team will want to make their colleagues' output better. They will be supportive of the individual, but they will be willing and able to challenge the issue vigorously.

FEEDBACK SHOULD BE GIVEN AT HIGH CADENCE

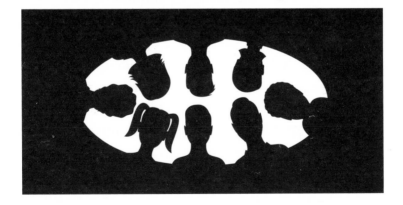

Growing up with two school teachers as parents, life was one big 'feedback loop'. My mum would shower me with feedback – on the go, in the car, in the moment. She was onto something, because feedback should be high-cadence and immediate. Don't save it all up for the annual appraisal – think of the 'after-action review' in the military or 'notes' given in a theatrical company. In a high-performance team, feedback is not only encouraged – it is demanded.

I was fortunate enough to spend an afternoon training with the Red Roses, England's women's rugby team. Watching them up close, I saw the head coaches and the players set out the context of a training session: the big picture, the main focus. Then the micro-coaching kicked in: the constant player-to-player review, the coach's 'whisper', the player-to-coach 'request'. Emily Scarratt, Katy Daley-Mclean and Natasha 'Mo' Hunt are all black belts at high-cadence, uber-relevant feedback, and they're always tweaking and refining. I saw no defensiveness, just a group of brilliant women trying to get better.

There's a particular kind of teammate whose objective is less about giving constructive feedback and more about trying to look smart. These people eat up time. One senior executive of a big multinational once said to me: 'We'd grow faster if we reduced the average IQ at the top of this company by 40 points.'

According to many of the companies I speak to, the shift to remote working in 2020 produced some interesting changes in workplace behaviour, one being that decision-making got faster. There was less 'grandstanding' and meetings were shorter. There is something about having meetings over video that encourages people to speak only if they have something important to say. When we move back to working in offices, it might be worth observing the 'Zoom rule': if you wouldn't say it on a video call, don't say it in a face-to-face meeting. It's all well and good to think of a clever question, but you don't always have to ask it.

Giving feedback in the moment is good for the recipient, but it's also really good for the person who is giving it. Don't let things fester and bottle up advice that can be used immediately. So often, the tension in a relationship is caused by the things that are going unsaid rather than anything that has been said. Most problems in the workplace are easily fixed, once they've been tabled. It can be like removing a weight from your shoulders to explain to a colleague that they are doing something that is creating stress and frustration. If it's framed constructively and delivered with kindness and generosity, not only are you getting something off your chest, you are also helping to make that person better.

Feedback is a gift, so be generous with it.

We talked about the importance of acknowledging strengths and work-ons in Chapter 1. It is very powerful for the leader to share their work-ons with their direct reports. It shows vulnerability and candour, but most of all it tells your people that no one can be a gold medallist at every event. Your weakness might be a teammate's strength, and vice versa. That's the beauty of a well-constructed team packed with complementary difference.

However, work-ons do come with a caveat: I always urge executives to put 'just enough' focus on them, and no more. I've watched people get so obsessed with the bits of their game that they wanted to improve that they stopped spending time and energy on the things they were great at. A high-performing team needs a range of people with different super-strengths – you can't all be world class at everything. What matters is that you've got everything covered. Focusing too much time and energy on your work-ons, and neglecting your strengths, will be detrimental to the business, the team and the individual.

My worst year on a rugby pitch was with Harlequins in 2005, the year we were relegated from the Premiership. Everyone in the team wanted to stay up, but our confidence was shot. Instead of remembering what we were good at, everything became focused on what we 'mustn't' and 'couldn't' do, collectively and individually.

Our spirits were crushed. Fear gripped us, because all the noise from the coaching team took the form of feedback that highlighted our work-ons. Our gradual decline was based around negativity and self-doubt, and the result was a self-fulfilling prophecy. We'd focused so much on our work-ons that we'd forgotten to celebrate our strengths.

Too much challenging feedback can paralyse a person, especially if they are young and hearing misaligned messages from a range of different sources. It can all get too much for a young athlete to compute. How often do you hear of someone giving up a sport because they've lost their love for it? As with all things, a balance is required. I've definitely seen kids get over-coached and watched them lose their instinctive feel for the game while they try to juggle a tsunami of feedback. Anyone who has stood over a golf ball with multiple 'swing thoughts' going through their head will know that it never ends well.

FEEDBACK REQUIRES A SPEEDY RESPONSE

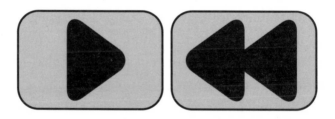

'Delivering feedback is always a balancing act; it should be challenging but kind, it should address work-ons but build on strengths and it should be high-cadence but not overwhelming.'

But feedback also requires a response. There is no point in asking for feedback and then ignoring it, just as there are few things more frustrating than seeing someone waste high-quality feedback that could help them grow.

Anyone who has bought a product online, called a customer service centre or simply opened an app on their smartphone will be familiar with customer feedback forms. It seems that every business is desperate for high-cadence feedback, yet we see a lot of companies who are drowning in customer feedback but choose not to respond to ongoing issues.

Many organisations like to think of themselves as customer-centric, but they are mistaking knowledge of the customer for commitment to serving them. Dave Lewis, former CEO of Tesco, says, 'The customer tells you everything you need to know. The key question for the CEO then becomes: "How do we change the business to serve the customer better?"'

True customer-centricity requires you to act on the data and insight that you receive. It's easy to talk about customer-centricity, but to genuinely have a customer-centric agenda at the heart of your culture is much harder.

Throughout my career, I've prided myself on my ability to use feedback to get better. I was highly coachable. I worked on my strengths and my work-ons. I wanted experts to point at the bits of my game that weren't good enough, no matter how uncomfortable that was. Andy Robinson helped with my work at the breakdown; Phil Larder helped my tackling; Dave Reddin focused on my conditioning. I owe a debt of thanks to these master craftsmen.

Now that I'm coaching rugby at Maidenhead RFC and for the last five years have taught maths up to GCSE level, I've become very aware that some people are more coachable than others. A student or a player who is hungry for feedback and open to learning makes the coaching role much more rewarding. A sponge mentality means having an openness and willingness to try new things without always knowing where they might lead. You might prefer to call it a 'growth mindset'.

KEEP LISTENING AND KEEP LEARNING

The first time I heard the phrase 'growth mindset', I was in my favourite Indian restaurant with my children. I was offered a menu, but said, 'No need for a menu, thanks. Lamb dhansak, please!'

'Why do you always have the same thing, Dad?'

'Because I love lamb dhansak.'

'Well, that's not very growth mindset.'

I resolved to look up the term as soon as I got home. And when I did, I learned that the concept came from the American academic Carol Dweck, a professor at Stanford and author of *Mindset: The New Psychology of Success*. She writes:

'In a growth mindset, people believe that their most basic abilities can be developed through dedication and hard work – brains and talent are just the starting point. This view creates a love of learning and resilience that is essential for great accomplishment.'

In a growth mindset, you are not only open to trying new things, but you have a more enlightened approach to failure because you focus on the learning rather than just the result. In contrast, with a fixed mindset, an individual has learned systems and protocols that work for them and which they tend to repeat.

These archetypes tend to be better at quality control than quality creation.

It's not as straightforward as saying that a growth mindset is good and a fixed one is bad, but it is fair to say that a fixed mindset is ill-suited to periods of dramatic change. An organisation should have a blend of both. There will be periods of dramatic change for any business, but there will also be periods when you just have to trade. It's possible for an organisation or culture to reach a point of 'transformation fatigue'. When there has been so much change, a period of stability is required. At these moments, people with a more fixed mindset can become valuable.

Dan Carter is an All Blacks legend and one of the greatest fly halves ever to play rugby. He has some fascinating insights into how a world-beating team like New Zealand uses feedback. 'It was understood that we were always growing the team,' he says. 'To be elite, you must have a growth mindset. Our best meetings were always when players were vulnerable – this is key to giving and receiving good feedback. You need to express your feelings, to say what you think and feel. We would signal that we were about to have a difficult conversation, but it would also be made clear that afterwards, no matter how tough the conversation was, we would walk out as mates, and we would commit. Steve Hansen [the coach] was brilliant at creating this environment and showing everyone that we could always get better. In a post-game review, he would often pick out me and Richie [McCaw], even when other players had made far more mistakes, to show everyone that nobody was above receiving feedback. No player was greater than the team. You needed big shoulders to have difficult conversations; you discuss, agree, commit, then move on. That was what was expected, whether you had one Test cap or 100. I left the All Blacks presuming that every team did that. I quickly learned that they didn't.'

Satya Nadella, the CEO of Microsoft, is a huge believer in the growth mindset. He said that he was trying to change Microsoft from being a 'know-it-all organisation to a learn-it-all organisation'. On his watch, Microsoft's share price has quadrupled.

Sir Clive Woodward was an exponent of the growth mindset long before the phrase had entered the mainstream, and so were our team. We gave and received feedback relentlessly. Phil Larder, our defensive coach, even gave us feedback after the World Cup final. He told me that I'd made fifteen tackles and missed one. I know exactly which one I missed – Stirling Mortlock had stepped inside, caught my weak arm and Wilko swept it up on my inside left. Why does that still annoy me? We won. Who cares? The team never played again. But I did care, and I still do.

Phil knew that a new-look England side would be playing in the Six Nations in three months' time, and that the other teams would prize the scalp of the world champions even more greatly. Staying ahead was a challenge that began immediately – and we would come to learn that staying at the top was even harder than getting there.

As a team, we listened, learned and were always prepared to fail. There was a disastrous experiment to drive rather than fly to Paris for a Five Nations game. The idea was that avoiding air travel would deliver us in a better mental and physical state for game day. But we hit terrible traffic after 20 minutes and it was a disaster: we arrived frustrated, tired and ill-prepared for the contest ahead.

But that restless nature also led to us working with Dr Sherylle Calder, better known as the Eye Doctor. The eye is a muscle, so why not train it to be better? Through training our eyes we became much better at seeing space and finding opportunity. Our search for the 1 per cent improvements would blow your mind. But both the approaches we adopted and the ones we threw out were collective calls. What might look great from the touchline doesn't always work on the field. And unless you can feed that back in, you are beaten before you start.

Cultures of excellence are cultures of learning, places where individuals are hungry for knowledge and candid about how they are trying to improve. They will declare their work-ons to their teammates free from fear, knowing that they will be asked to give coaching to and receive coaching from their peers. A good leader will teach, grow their people and lift as they climb. They will create a safe space for their direct reports to be candid. They will ask good questions and, crucially, they will be great listeners.

Dave Lewis spent the first 27 years of his career at Unilever, where he developed his listening skills at a highly accelerated rate. 'When you go abroad in an expat posting, your ears and your eyes become your most important assets,' he says. 'You need to be brutally objective. I like thinking about the first 90 days when I start a new job: the first 30 days are for listening and asking naive questions, the next 30 days for checking that you have understood and asking "what-ifs", and the final 30 days should be spent working up the plan and the proposals.'

From Dave Lewis to Damian Lewis: when I spoke to the star of *Billions*, *Homeland* and *Band of Brothers* for my podcast, I asked him about the best advice he'd ever been given with regards to acting. This was his response:

In terms of advice for acting, and particularly stage acting, it is listening. Of course, we're all used to actors banging on and talking, but the secret to unleashing great acting and true spontaneity is listening absolutely in the moment, so that your response to everything that you hear is genuine, spontaneous, fresh and newly minted. And if you're in the theatre for a long run, you might do a hundred performances of a play. Just forcing yourself to strip everything else away and be absolutely still and concentrate on what the person is saying to you will generate the most honest, truthful and, therefore, vibrant response. Which, of course, is what the audience then become a part of. So nothing is choreographed, nothing is preordained, nothing is contrived or manufactured, that's how you keep acting fresh and spontaneous. What happens when you have a group of people in a space listening intently to each other is, something odd happens, the space closes. It closes because it becomes more and more intimate and then the theatre, the audience, close in with you, and the whole thing becomes a more precise and more nuanced experience than just the bluster of speaking. Which is actually what I really love to do.

Damian is describing listening as a mechanism for feedback. He gives his fellow actors feedback as they perform, second by second, and he also gives them his complete respect, attention and focus. I'm not sure you can give any greater gifts.

World-Class Feedback: Highlights

1. Be tough on the issue, but soft on the person – challenging feedback can be delivered with kindness.

2. With feedback, context is everything – create a contract whereby everyone understands that feedback is given with the intention of growing the individual first and then the company.

3. Don't bottle it all up for the annual appraisal. Be generous with your feedback – it should be a daily habit, not an annual chore.

4. High-quality, high-cadence feedback demands action. Use it, and you will grow. It's rude not to accept a gift, after all.

5. Feedback is a balancing act: focus on your strengths more than your work-ons.

6. Don't shoot the messenger – really listen to feedback, while understanding that it is only being delivered in the hope of making you better.

7. Be a 'learn-it-all' rather than a 'know-it-all'.

3. Innovation

'Elite cultures are cultures of ideas, places where brave thinking takes place and where visionary leaders innovate and experiment.'

DIFFERENCE TOGETHERNESS GROWTH

The Carthaginian general Hannibal was one of the great leaders of antiquity. He famously took his elephants across the Alps to defeat the Romans, who had expected a challenge by sea and never dreamed that an invader would come from the north.

The England team I played in would always try to do something in a game that would surprise our opponents. We called it a 'Hannibal call'. We would come up with a move or a pattern to run, typically as early as possible in games, that would have our opponents scratching their heads. It wasn't designed with the sole purpose of scoring – although that would be a bonus – but it was intended to create uncertainty, doubt and indecision, and to help us take the initiative.

A great example of a Hannibal call was in the World Cup final in 2003 – though this one was atypical in that it came late in the game. Deep in extra time, with moments left on the clock, we had an attacking lineout just outside the Aussie 22-metre line. Our lineout leader Ben Kay's job was to instruct the hooker, Steve Thompson, where to throw the ball, and he had three options: he could go with himself in the middle, Martin Johnson, our banker, at the front, or Lewis Moody at the back. The most unlikely call of the three was the one to 'Mad Dog' Moody. Not only was it the longest and hardest throw for Thompson to execute, Moody had only just come on, and he was being lifted by the diminutive Neil Back. The Aussies were preparing for the throw to Johnson or Kay; nobody expected Thompson to throw all the way to the back. It was a ballsy call, made under the most extreme pressure, and it was executed perfectly, with a pinpoint throw and a flawless lift and catch. What resulted three rucks later was the drop goal that closed out the game; I think Hannibal would have approved.

Elite cultures are cultures of ideas, where brave thinking takes place and visionary leaders innovate and experiment. These are environments where, despite a hierarchy and structure, ideas can come from anywhere. There is a growth mindset and individuals are encouraged to try new things.

Ben spent 24 years at BBH, including 16 as CEO. Celebrating difference and encouraging creative thinking was the cultural keystone of the business, and this philosophy was embodied by the corporate identity of the 'black sheep'. BBH always tried to create advertising for clients that was very different from the competition, and the leadership group tried to create a very different kind of advertising agency and to hire very different types of people. In 2016, they ran the simple recruitment ad, 'Black Sheep Wanted'. One of BBH's core beliefs is simply: 'We believe in the power of creativity and the primacy of the idea.'

This philosophical commitment to difference was born of a fundamental belief that advertising that is different will cut through more effectively and work harder for clients.

One of BBH's clients was Alexis Nasard, who was global CMO of Heineken. Alexis was subsequently CEO of the huge footwear company Bata and is now CEO of Kantar, a marketing research giant with 30,000 employees in over 100 countries. He makes a wonderful point about the role of innovation: 'Innovation is such a great and noble pursuit because when it works well, everybody wins. The consumer wins, the retailer wins, the category wins, the competition and the economy wins. That's why innovation is so important. That's why it's so special.'

Great innovation is an accelerator of growth, but it's also an accelerator of change – new products and ideas will often require new capabilities and new people. It will help you to diversify and to reinvent the core business. It will help you to serve existing customers with new products and services, and it will help you to find new ones.

So, what is the role of innovation and brave creative thinking on the journey to excellence and growth?

FRESH EYES ACCELERATE INNOVATION

Humphrey Walters is a celebrated public speaker, adventurer and businessman. He had no real idea about rugby, but he knew a heck of a lot about how to increase the quality of performance from elite teams. He always offered Sir Clive Woodward's England a fresh perspective on challenges we were facing on and off the pitch, and he ended up completely changing our half-time protocols.

As a young team, one of our problems was that we often started the second half of a match poorly. Humphrey's brilliantly simple idea was for us to change into fresh kit at half-time. Why? Because the process would create a break in our routine, and in a clean white kit you can't help but feel like a million dollars. This simple innovation was the catalyst for other ideas. Changing our kit led to a quieter first two minutes of the break: our heart rates slowed down, our thoughts were more composed and the delivery of the half-time message was much improved – as was the quality of our listening. One simple idea had morphed into a whole new half-time protocol. A seemingly small idea had become the catalyst for something much more transformational.

Donald Rumsfeld, the former US secretary of defense, famously made a fascinating set of distinctions around different types of knowledge. He says that 'there are known knowns', the things that we know we know. Then 'there are known unknowns', the things we know we don't know. But there are also 'unknown unknowns', the things that we don't know we don't know. When it comes to innovation, organisations need different people and different ways of thinking to compensate for the things they know they don't know. Organisational beliefs and orthodoxies can be perpetuated long after they are relevant or even true. They can outlive their 'sell-by date', and they need to be reviewed, challenged and revised.

Andy Fennell, formerly of Diageo, develops this idea further: 'To have a truly disruptive view, you need different inputs and different people. We knew that asking people who had trained and grown up inside Diageo to have a new world view was not going to be successful – that's why we set up Distill Ventures. We invested in entrepreneurs who we really believed in, but who actively disagreed with our world view. You need an innovation model that doesn't allow the white corpuscles of the organisation to kill new and different ideas.'

You need men and women from outside your circle of trust who offer a different perspective. Otherwise, you eventually end up assimilating, agreeing and slowly but surely stifling one another's imagination and growth. Crucially, you need to learn how best to marshall your resources to offer the best hope of innovation.

DON'T NEGLECT YOUR CORE

To create genuine innovation on a sports pitch is very hard. We spent years trying to perfect the cross-field kick and catch as an offensive weapon. Our wingers would line up outside the pitch, almost touching the stands, and run a line from out to in, attacking blind spots on the flanks and stretching defences in the midfield. We often practised this, but never at the expense of our basics: the scrum, the lineout and defence. Working on your performance basics is rarely the most exciting part of any training session, but it might be the most important. Any team or business that neglects its core skills will pay a heavy price.

All businesses need to make sure that they are both performing and transforming, respecting the core but also future-proofing themselves. Good businesses sweat their existing assets and capabilities while also building new ones. The key for every business is to make sure that they are applying the appropriate levels of energy and resource to these two critical agendas. Neglect the transformation agenda, and you will fail to evolve your business; neglect the performance agenda, and the core business will wither and die. Both agendas require top talent, leadership focus and attention; they are both strategic imperatives.

From 2011 to 2013, BBH's core business was doing so well that the innovation and diversification agenda was pushed to the back-burner. The leadership team did not 'mend the roof while the sun was shining' because they were too busy beating their financial plans and driving their core business ever harder. Then, when the core business lost momentum in 2014, the team had to accelerate the transformation plays that they had neglected. Innovation became a strategic priority and diversification became a necessity. The positive end to this story is that by 2018, half of BBH's profits were being delivered by businesses that Ben and his team had set up in 2014: BBH Sport, BBH Health and BBH X. BBH had performed and transformed.

The composition of your innovation team is critical, and complementary difference is once again key. Dave Lewis, formerly of Tesco says: 'The best innovation teams at Tesco were always a blend of people who knew the operation and people from the outside. If you ask operators to innovate while running the operation, the operation will always take priority. The best things we did happened when we took small, blended teams out of the business and focused them on innovation.'

Of course, knowing which ideas to select for resourcing and exploration is a critical leadership skill. Innovation is expensive, and you can burn cash and time in new product development at an alarming rate. The ability to edit and focus is a leadership skill of profound value. Too often, the leadership team will be driving too many agendas and chasing too many 'strategic imperatives'. Innovation, like strategy, requires you to make choices.

NOT MANY IDEAS ARE BORN PERFECT

Good ideas iterate and evolve. Like a baton, they are passed around the group and made better over time. People who are great at having ideas are not always great at crafting and improving them, and vice versa. Some people are brilliant builders but less good at starting the creative process off. We come back to difference once again, because the team required to resource your innovation unit needs to be a melting pot of different cognitive archetypes. You need people who really understand the product and the technology, as well as those who really understand the consumer. You want some classic starters and some great builders and finishers, as well as people with strong commercial skills and maybe a few rogue thinkers to shake things up.

In his brilliant book *Creativity, Inc.*, the Pixar co-founder Ed Catmull describes the concept of the company's 'brain trust'. What the leadership group at Pixar learned over time was that no matter how experienced the team working on a movie, there would be a moment when they would get stuck. It could be to do with the narrative, a character's development or it could be a technical issue. What they learned was that it almost always

51

required some fresh eyes and an intervention from outside the team to get things moving again.

The genius of The Braintrust was its governance. You took your problem to the great and the good of Pixar, and they made suggestions and proposals; nothing was a directive. You walked in owning the problem, you received feedback and you walked out owning the solution. Core to its whole reason for being is the understanding that ideas evolve, stumble and might even grind to a shuddering halt. You need leaders who understand this, and teams who are confident enough to ask for help. Ed Catmull says, 'We rely on The Braintrust to push towards excellence and to root out mediocrity. It is our primary delivery system for straight talk. Its premise is simple: put smart, passionate people in a room together, charge them with identifying and solving problems and encourage them to be candid.'

Under Eddie Jones, the England rugby team start with an idea of how to beat a team and then they refine it. Eddie gives his playmakers the big idea and then he lets them iterate, refine and master the execution. There is a relentlessness to the way they stress test and practise. They recreate the game environment, with players and balls flying everywhere, until the shapes, movements and timings become almost second nature. The mistakes made on the training pitch are a critical part of the process. The England midfield know what perfection looks like because they've fallen short a thousand times. In the opening seconds of their epic win over New Zealand in the 2019 World Cup semifinal, all their work came to wonderful fruition. George Ford reacted to a defensive mistake from New Zealand and put Elliot Daly into space. He skipped past Richie Mo'unga and England were in behind the All Blacks. Moments later, Manu Tuilagi scored. England had iterated, refined and executed perfectly when it mattered most.

SOMETIMES THE BIG INNOVATION IS YOUR SELECTION

Gary Neville, part of the legendary Class of '92 at Manchester United, told me about the bold selection innovations at the football club: 'Two key things that Sir Alex Ferguson did was around the use of the squad and backing youth. Football had always been about 11 players with one sub in the 1970s and 1980s, but Ferguson was soon shifting the numbers around, so that he was then able to manage a 22-man squad. He had four number one strikers in the treble season in 1999 – Teddy Sheringham, Ole Gunnar Solskjaer, Andrew Cole and Dwight Yorke – and he kept them all happy and engaged. Sir Alex was the first manager to use young players and introduce them to first-team football in the domestic cups. In the "Ryan Giggs" FA Cup semifinal against Arsenal in 1999 [Giggs beat about six players to score a wonder goal and then took his shirt off and whirled it above his head], that was actually a replay on the Wednesday night, having played Arsenal four days before. Ferguson made seven changes to his team from Saturday to Wednesday because he knew he couldn't get 100 per cent out of the same group.'

Succession planning is talked about a lot in business, but it's rarely executed with the commitment or bravery that Sir Alex demonstrated with the Class of '92. At the core of his selection was the belief that 'if you're good enough, you're old enough.' He was making bets for the long term. These players would do their apprenticeship on the biggest stage, and they would grow together.

Ben was 30 when he was made CEO of BBH in Asia Pacific. He then spent four years running one of BBH's smaller businesses, in advance of running the mother ship, BBH London, for twelve. Back in 2002, this was succession management executed in a highly strategic fashion. Ben was given the platform and opportunity to develop his leadership skills in a business delivering 10 per cent of the group's profit, before running a business that delivered 50 per cent. It was a bold selection by BBH's leadership because they knew that some people would regard Ben's age and inexperience as an issue.

Eddie Jones talks about how much he learned from 1991 World Cup-winning Wallaby coach Bob Dwyer when it came to picking young players. Dwyer's philosophy was simple: if a new player is going to be better than the player you have currently, pick them straight away. They will not be the finished article on day one, but it's a trade-off worth taking. Eddie says he saw Tom Curry as an 18-year-old and decided that he had to take him on tour to Argentina and cap him straight away. He knew that he would be a superstar, and he knew international game time was the only way to fast-track him.

It takes some bravery to make a call like that, and as we'll see, courage is necessary for innovation.

BIG IDEAS REQUIRE COURAGE

In a team packed with complementary difference, there will be a number of approaches to solving problems. Although there will be some who naturally tend towards a cautious approach, which is an important perspective in any decision, it is vital for innovation if there is courage in the ranks – particularly among the leadership team.

In the final of the men's coxless four at the 2004 Olympic Games in Athens, Matthew Pinsent, James Cracknell, Ed Coode and Steve Williams devised a plan that seemed like racing suicide. Cracknell's idea was to race as if the finish line were at the 1,900 metre mark rather than at the full 2 kilometres. He proposed that they gamble everything and empty the tank with 100 metres still to go because for them, it was gold or nothing. 'The last 100 will look after itself,' he said.

What happened next is the stuff of legend. The crew started their final surge far earlier than normal, caught their opponents off-guard and hung on desperately for gold. It was an incredibly brave piece of thinking that required tremendous mental and physical courage. I asked Pinsent to tell me more about this critical moment and the discussions that took place around it. 'We knew that it was gamble to get the gold, to build a truly audacious plan in the last stage, and that if it didn't work it could lose us every medal,' he says. 'We made a pledge the night before that we wanted to be able to look each other in the eye for the rest of our lives and know that we had given everything, way more than we wanted to celebrate a silver medal.'

Companies try to mitigate risk with the use of research and data, but the biggest innovation still requires tremendous courage. Think of the moment when Richard Branson, owner of a music business in Virgin Records, rolled the dice and chose to build an airline, or when Apple stopped new product development on everything but the iPhone, iPad and iPod. It is often the fierce resolve of a founder, or the instincts of a leader who is at their core a risk-taker, that allows these iconic moves to take place.

INNOVATION IS A FORCE MULTIPLIER

Today's military commanders don't have elephants to deploy in the field. They have a far more powerful weapon: technology. A contact in the special forces told me how technology is used as a 'force multiplier': 'I can be deep in enemy territory, controlling multiple drone assets, in support of daily airstrikes, while also capturing imagery that will improve our situational awareness. This technology allows us to move troops, at greater pace and with lower casualty rates.' A mash-up of new technology and enduring combat skills is a potent combination in the field. The special forces understand, just as many great businesses do, that technology shouldn't replace human beings; it should amplify and accelerate our capabilities.

Juxtapositions and unusual partnerships are often at the heart of innovation. The fashion and retail icon Paul Smith once gave an entire presentation on colours that shouldn't work together, but do. It's a principle that sits at the heart of his design philosophy, and it has powered his business and brand. The iconic Paul Smith sock is a perfect example of 'difference and togetherness'.

Headspace is a company that delivers meditation and thousands of years' worth of ancient Buddhist philosophy in an utterly modern format. The CEO and co-founder Rich Pierson says, 'Technology is integrated into everything we do. It's not a separate element. The question we always ask is, "How can we use technology to help us deliver our vision? How can tech accelerate and amplify?" It's just too simplistic to say that tech is unhealthy or negative. It's our relationship with tech that can sometimes drive unhealthy behaviour. You have to meet people where they are, and technology is woven into everything we do – it's not separate. Tech is an enabler. The best tech, in my opinion, is when it's invisible to the member or user. We like tech you can't see but which makes your experience of the service better, without you knowing how.'

Sir Clive Woodward never missed an opportunity to use technology to our advantage. Prozone was the forerunner of today's sat nav tracking devices that measure the distance travelled, the speed and even the power of individual hits. I soon worked out that my style of play didn't deliver big numbers – in fact, I was always near the bottom when it came to distance travelled – so I came up with a plan. As the TV cameras focused on Jonny Wilkinson during conversions, I would spend two minutes jogging from touchline to touchline, and I rocketed up the leader board. Clive had innovated, but so had I.

INNOVATION IS ART AND SCIENCE

Entrepreneurs understand the importance of innovation. It's why they are often invited to collaborate with big businesses – particularly those that are stuck in a certain type of mindset. I asked Sarah Willingham about the characteristics that make for a great entrepreneur: 'I've found that so much of the dream and vision of an entrepreneur is intuitive. Founders often have a clear sense of what the business will become, but the really good entrepreneurs have a flexible mindset. They are able to react and pivot. They are also painfully optimistic, which is often what keeps them going in the face of multiple setbacks.' These are all good characteristics for anyone trying to innovate: optimism, flexibility, intuition and resilience.

Many of the athletes who are judged by history to have been the most creative and innovative are largely misunderstood. The bit of their game that most people miss is that, as well as being more naturally gifted than their contemporaries, they also work harder.

The more I reflect on innovation, the more I believe that great ideas require industry *and* creativity. They require people who know everything about the organisation and people who know nothing. Like so many things in life, it's a case of **and not or**. For businesses and teams to perform, they need people who are constantly thinking of new things and people who are brilliant at delivering the old thing. They will need creative thinkers and operational thinkers, those who can deliver on strategy and those who can execute.

At the heart of many of the great innovation stories is a group of people with different skills, trying to develop very different ideas. Because innovation is both an art *and* a science, it requires rigour *and* creativity. It is about listening to what the consumer tells you, but also taking them to places they haven't yet imagined. Akio Morita, the legendary co-founder of Sony, famously said: 'The public does not know what is possible, but we do.' Henry Ford went even further: 'If I had asked people what they wanted, they'd have said faster horses.'

World-Class Innovation: Highlights

1. If you want to accelerate innovation, get different perspectives.

2. Innovation is rarely a light-bulb eureka moment. Let 'Iterate, refine, execute' be your mantra.

3. Don't neglect your core, and don't get distracted by innovation projects that will not materially impact the business.

4. If you're good enough, you're old enough. Sometimes a bold selection can be the big innovation.

5. Innovation isn't for the faint-hearted – it requires courage. Optimism, flexibility, intuition and resilience will come in handy, too.

6. Mash up the old and the new. Technology can be your 'force multiplier', even if the core of your business is an ancient meditation practice.

7. The magic, as ever, is in the blend. Successful businesses need people who are constantly thinking of new things as well as those who are consistently delivering the old things.

4. Decision-Making

'High-performance teams leverage different perspectives and harvest the collective wisdom of the group.'

DIFFERENCE   TOGETHERNESS   GROWTH

When I interviewed Richie Mo'unga, the All Blacks fly half, he told me a revealing story about his first few Tests. He explained that he had been so concerned about not making any mistakes that he wrote all the key moves on his forearm. He'd never done this before, at any level, but the pressure of international rugby had got to him and he'd made a small but significant change to his process. For the first time in his playing career, he was following a playbook – and his head was down, not up.

After playing a number of Tests, he came to realise that on game day, having done all of his prep, he needed to get his head up and play what he saw. He needed to trust his instincts, as he had throughout his career. This was a man who had steered his club side, the Crusaders, to a hat-trick of titles. A player that I coached for the Barbarians had suddenly become a slave to what was written on his forearm when his eyes and his gut had always been his key weapons.

In the world of leadership development and training, decision-making is a skill that is often neglected. In sport, I would argue that decision-making is one of the key differences between a good player and a great one. The great player will make good choices under the greatest pressure and on the biggest of days. Someone like Mo'unga might look like he's playing purely on instinct, the truth is that, just as with any other skill, decision-making can be developed, improved and mastered. It is something that can get better with experience.

Leaders need to build their own systems and protocols for decision-making. They need to create their own network of advisers, and they need to be able to decide how much time and rigour different types of decisions require. Because decisions, like people, come in different shapes and sizes.

Let's explore some of the things we've learned about decision-making at the highest level of sport and business.

MASTER YOUR CORE SKILLS SO THAT YOU CAN TRUST YOUR INSTINCTS

During my school and university days, my dad would always say, 'You can't be creative or instinctive without absolute mastery of your core skills.' He never stopped stressing his belief that my core skills were the foundation of everything. It is a simple philosophy, though it isn't always one a young player wants to hear. Working on your basics can be monotonous and tiresome, but it is the platform upon which your whole game will be built. For your core skills to hold up under extreme pressure, you need to know that they are rock solid. It's a philosophy that is endorsed by rugby legend Dan Carter. 'In the All Blacks, we always wanted to make sure that we did the basics, the core roles and skills, better than anyone else,' he says. 'We'd practise the same stuff a seven-year-old would.' Doing the basics better than anyone else is a simple but often overlooked strategy for building competitive advantage.

At the start of your international career your basics will be scrutinised and tested. Talking to Richie Mo'unga reminded me of my first few internationals. I was offered plenty of advice, most of which was along the lines of 'Play your natural game' and 'Play like you play for your club.' Yet when it came down to it, nothing felt the same. The speed of the game, the power of the hits, the lung-bursting intensity – it was on a completely different level. Just when you should be relying on all your hours of training and trusting your instincts, you end up trying to avoid making mistakes. It was only after around 15 to 20 caps that I started to believe that I deserved to be wearing an international jersey. Lots of players do not get that kind of an apprenticeship. At the heart of my growing self-belief, there was an awareness that my skills were holding up under the most extreme pressure. My confidence grew, the imposter syndrome diminished and my mindset shifted, allowing me to really start to play.

Confidence is absolutely central to great decision-making. Not over-confidence, of course, but a belief in your judgement, your own process and cognitive capability. I've always believed that there is a direct correlation between the work you do in advance of the big day and your ability to turn up feeling confident. Your 'instincts' are honed over thousands of hours of practice.

If you've role-played a scenario or experienced it live before, your ability to make good decisions at high speed will be increased. Think of a big speech or presentation. If you've cut corners and skimped on your preparation, you'll stand in front of your audience feeling nervous, and rightly so. But if you've put the hours in, you'll have faith in your content and feel ready to deliver. Every minute spent crafting your material is another down payment of confidence that you are investing in yourself. It is money in the bank.

An experienced operator in the workplace will draw on their experience to make decisions. They will have the visible data in front of them, but they will also have captured reams of invisible data during their career. Their instincts will have been honed through good times and bad. They might make a decision in 30 minutes, but those 30 minutes might be backed up with 30 years of experience, and there are no shortcuts to building this kind of muscle memory.

You can't magically create 30 years of experience, so how do you approach your decision-making if you can't call upon this kind of leadership mileage? How do you project confidence and clarity when you are making big calls for the first time?

As BBH CEO in Asia, Ben found himself in a new market with a new leadership team, trying to engage Asian clients and consumers whom he knew little about. It would have been easy for him to lose his confidence and start to question his decision-making, but he committed to a mental process of telling himself relentlessly that he simply needed to do the things that he'd always done, just on a bigger stage. He had led highly successful teams in London – he just needed to do the same things at greater scale. He had no CEO experience, but he did have plenty of client, creative and commercial experience. So he made his inner monologue relentlessly positive, choosing to constantly reaffirm to himself that he deserved to be there. Like a Test match batsman in cricket, you just need to get through those first few overs, trusting your technique and the processes that have got you to that position. Making dramatic changes is a very dangerous game. Over time, you'll learn which bits of your game you need to change, but while you're building a score, you need to stick to playing a few trusted shots that you know.

The positivity and generosity of your inner voice matters hugely in these big jobs, not least because there will always be plenty of people willing to tell you how they think things should be done.

'In a job like this, you'll get lots of advice,' says Dave Lewis of Tesco. 'That advice will never be aligned, by the way, so you've always got to keep some perspective. And trust your instincts. Instincts honed over years and years of practice. Instinct with no skill or experience is gambling.'

Every sport and every business has some 'basics'. These need to be articulated and worked on relentlessly because they are the foundations upon which everything else is built. For many elite performers, it is not their ability to do extraordinary things that marks them out; it's their ability to do the ordinary things extraordinarily well.

In rugby, a basic or core skill might be passing. In a business career, it might be building client relationships. These skills never cease to matter, regardless of how senior or experienced you become. They are your foundations as a graduate trainee or a CEO. This stuff is rarely sexy or exciting – it's the stuff that the kids often find boring – but it's also the stuff that pays the bills and builds careers.

CREATE A COMPASS FOR DECISION-MAKING

Wayne Hoyle is a former special forces soldier with more than 30 years of experience. In 2018, I was one of eight adventurers who went with him to the North Pole on a fundraising expedition led by three special forces guys, a ten-day test of character. Right from the start, Wayne's presence gave us all confidence. He exuded a calm and reassuring energy. As long as I could see him, everything was fine. I watched him make hundreds of decisions on that trip. He seemed to make them quickly, and without too much fuss or discussion. At the end of the trip, I asked him about his decision-making process and he gave me a brutally simple answer:

> Whether I have a second, an hour or a week, my basic process remains the same. There are two considerations: by making this decision, am I moving closer to achieving the aim, or the aim of my commander? And am I doing what is best for my team?

Wayne uses those two simple questions as his compass for decision-making, giving himself a system to make consistently good decisions.

Olympians will tell you that during a four-year cycle, it can sometimes feel like you are a long way from the event. Finding motivation can be challenging, and individual daily decisions can feel quite dislocated from your performance on the big day.

Kate Richardson-Walsh talks powerfully about how the GB women's hockey team she captained at the 2016 Olympics took their purpose of 'win gold' and gave it everyday application in the years, months and weeks leading up to the tournament by turning it into a simple question: would a gold medallist do that? 'Would a gold medallist eat that croissant? Probably not. Would a gold medallist put another ten kilos on the squat rack? They probably would.'

It's a brilliantly simple piece of thinking that creates a compass for decision-making. It gave the four-year goal daily application and proximity, connecting short-term decisions to the long-term goal.

Ben once saw Francis Ford Coppola – director of 'The God-father' trilogy and *Apocalypse Now* – talk about his decision-making process. He explained how a director on a film set has a hundred decisions to make every day. What lens? What angle? What lighting? What performance? To help him make these decisions, Coppola would reduce the essence of his films down to a single word. If he had this distillation of the whole movie in his head, it would help govern all of his decisions – it would be his North Star. Fittingly, his word for *The Godfather* was 'succession'.

Coppola is essentially crafting a 'purpose' for his film, just as businesses do, and the impact can be profound. One of the first things that Dave Lewis did as CEO of Tesco was rewrite the purpose of the UK's biggest retailer. He chose the following words: 'Serving Britain's shoppers a little better every day.' It was impressive to see how that sentence quickly penetrated the business and became a compass for decision-making in every department and at every level. When an idea was presented in a meeting, someone would ask, 'Will this help us to serve Britain's shoppers a little better every day?' If the answer was yes, they did it; if the answer was no, they didn't. The purpose had become a question and it had entered the corporate vocabulary.

THE 40–70 RULE

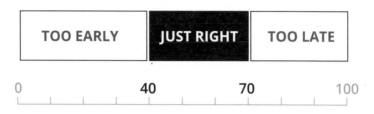

THE DATA IN YOUR POSSESSION

Colin Powell is a former four-star general, national security adviser, and chairman of the joint chiefs of staff – the highest position in the US Armed Forces. He also served as US secretary of state between 2001 and 2005 during George W. Bush's presidency. Powell developed a theory that a commander in the field should make their decisions while in possession of between 40 and 70 per cent of the available data. He argues that with less than 40 per cent you don't have enough information, and with more than 70 per cent you're acting too late.

We will all have worked with people who make their decisions at either extreme of this spectrum, and both can be frustrating and dangerous: one lacks rigour and the other creates paralysis. In a team you need people who want to open a question up and others who want to close it down, some people who are instinctive and others who are more data-driven.

Dave Lewis had a sufficient level of information to take the many decisions he had to make at Tesco. 'I don't need to be the expert, but I do need to know enough,' he says. 'Once you've got a purpose, the financial parameters and the right level of expertise around you, most decisions become relatively straightforward.'

A confident CEO will put people around them who have a

contrasting cognitive style, who will interrogate and challenge their thinking. These are people who might, in the short term, slow them down to pause for thought, but who in the long term will speed them up. If one leader always looks at problems through the 'commercial lens', it's important to put colleagues alongside them who think 'people first' or who focus on the implications for 'brand and reputation'. In pulling together the data required to make a decision, the task is not just to create the 40–70 window but to ensure the data sources are varied and complementary. You want a view of the whole battlefield, and no single perspective will ever give you that.

Pooling these views will require you to ask good questions and to really listen. As we talked about in the chapter on feedback, good listening skills are a prerequisite for a high-performance team, because they help the team make consistently good decisions. Bad listeners tend to make bad decisions.

HARVEST THE COLLECTIVE WISDOM OF THE GROUP

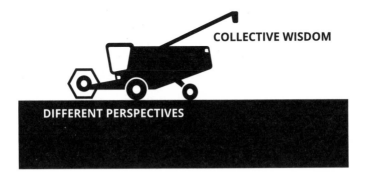

Sir Graham Henry is a very fine coach – he won a World Cup with New Zealand in 2011, after all. But on the British and

Irish Lions tour to Australia in 2001, some of us struggled with the way he operated. The relationship often felt like one between teacher and pupil, with a one-way flow of information and ideas.

We got off to a good start, when he let the backs run around for a couple of hours on the training pitch at the team hotel in Weybridge before we left the UK. We had some special players: Brian O'Driscoll, Jonny Wilkinson, Jason Robinson, Neil Jenkins, Rob Howley, Ronan O'Gara. It was a 'brains trust'. We experimented, playing seven vs seven, figuring out what we liked and what worked for us. We were loving being able to create our own playlist.

But then, once the session finished, the management asked us if we'd had a nice time and gave us the moves they wanted us to use for the tour. I know time was tight, but what a waste.

Once you've experienced a coach-to-player relationship in which there's a two-way transfer of knowledge and ideas, it's hard to go back to a teacher – pupil relationship. There's no point packing your team with difference and not allowing it to express itself. Philip Jansen, CEO of BT, makes exactly this point: 'Building the right amount of difference into your team comes with some challenges. You must create enough time for challenge and for debate. It's too easy when time is tight to default to people who think like you – you need to be open to learning and you need to run towards uncertainty. I'm always curious and I love learning – having a growth mindset is really important in the biggest jobs. You need to get comfortable with the things you don't know and with the acknowledgement that you will need people around you who know more than you.'

A warning sign for any leader who has been in a role for a significant length of time is the moment when they stop asking for input and advice, believing that they 'know' the market, the role or the competition. With experience comes wisdom, but the past is often a poor predictor of the future. An executive who is over-confident in their knowledge of a market is courting disaster because the business context changes constantly. A strategy that worked in one environment at one time may prove utterly unsuccessful when repeated. The challenge is often that context can change gradually, without you noticing.

If a leader is going to be in post for a long time, they need to make sure that their team is churned regularly. This kind of change in personnel allows the leader to balance stability with freshness, exposing players to new voices and ideas within a fixed framework and culture. This creates a positive tension that great leaders actively embrace. They know what to change and what to keep. They know which ideas and people have served their purpose and which ones should endure. This kind of approach can appear brutal when a long-time servant of an organisation or team is stood down, but it's a critical part of reinvention and succession management. It's how dynasties are built and how excellence is maintained beyond the career of specific individuals. A great side regenerates in flight with new talent brought in as older talent begins to wane. The culture is preserved and refreshed as senior players set standards and pass on good habits to the next generation.

Sir Alex Ferguson was brilliant at managing this, contrasting his own longevity with constant changes to his coaching staff, and it seems that Eddie Jones is adopting a similar strategy. He introduces new voices and ideas within a framework and identity that he sets.

Of course, any leader in this position will have to make the toughest decision of all: knowing when it's time to go, assuming that she or he is fortunate enough to decide on the timing of their departure. There is often a time window on the efficacy and impact of a CEO, because increased confidence and knowledge can blind them to a changing context. The quality of their decision-making can diminish as they take less notice of more challenging voices. Or worse still, they can remove the more challenging voices from their inner circle completely. The great skill is to spot the signals that the time is right to go: is there a leadership group ready to step up? Is the business ready for some fresh leadership voices and ideas? Is their energy for the mission beginning to wane?

YOU NEED PEOPLE IN THE ROOM WHO CAN MAKE THINGS HAPPEN

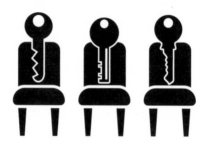

Andy Fennell, formerly of Diageo, makes the point that you don't just need difference in the room, you need people with the power and authority to make things happen:

> After the financial crisis, Diageo, like every business, was cutting costs. But we knew that it was the creation of new revenues that would power us forward. We did two things. We took growth ideas to the most senior team. If you need to make big plays, you need to speak to people who have the power to say yes. More than 50 per cent of our exec meetings during that period were focused on reviewing growth ideas. There was fear and nervousness in the markets, so the centre had to take the lead. We also invested £30 million in

leadership development. The Diageo share price tripled during that period – we created a growth mindset.

Andy is referring to Diageo's investment in the quality of leadership within the business and, crucially, the importance of getting the key decision-makers in the room. This might seem obvious, but in big organisations you often have to go through many layers of bureaucracy before a decision can be made. You are often faced by people who have the power to say no but not yes. Not only is this process slow and energy-sapping, but good ideas can be diluted as they endure a series of compromises. Speeding up organisational decision-making is often an exercise in taking away rather than adding. It's about removing stakeholders and processes to help you go faster.

Imagine you're a leader in the 40–70 window. You've harvested the collective wisdom of the group and it's time to make the call. How should you approach this final phase of the process? There are two important concepts to embrace:

- You should acknowledge that you might fail, and think through the consequences.
- You should liberate the emotional and rational part of your judgement process.

An experienced leader will understand that some decisions will go wrong – they realise that failure is an inevitable part of growth. The skill is not to avoid it, but to mitigate its impact. A leader who is scared to make a mistake will be paralysed in their decision-making. Sometimes it is helpful to simply ask yourself, 'What's the worst thing that can happen?' Take the time to scenario-plan the implications of your idea not working and think through how you can limit your exposure. A good leader does not fear failure; they just make sure it is not too expensive.

Once you've embraced the possibility of failure and mitigated your exposure, the final task for the leader is to liberate the rational and emotional parts of their judgement – and that brings us to fire and ice.

FIRE IN THE BELLY AND ICE IN THE BRAIN

I spoke with Jason Fox about his decision-making protocols under extreme pressure. 'On operations, as the leader, you're always one guy back, so that you have a full view of the action,' he says. 'If you see or feel something that's not quite right, that's when you have to step up. You need to make an intervention. It will be your job to say, "Slow down", "Take a moment" or "We need to make a change".'

To do this, you need the adrenalin and 'fire' to be at your most alert, but you also need the composure and 'ice' to slow things down. At the highest level of sport, everyone is talented, works hard and has the necessary physical attributes. But, as I identified at the beginning of this chapter, decision-making is a key difference between the good players and the great ones. I don't just mean captaincy or coaching decisions; I mean split-second decisions. Which man do I hit? Do I attempt that interception? Do I throw that pass or hang on?

It's incredibly hard to balance the passion and aggression required to play international rugby with the calmness and clarity of thought needed to make good decisions. Falling short on either dimension will limit your ability to perform. You are trying to find that perfect balance of fire and ice. Great players can find the emotional touchpoints needed for that perfect state, able to access and leverage head and heart.

I was introduced to the Russian psychologist Yuri Hanin in Po Bronson and Ashley Merryman's book *Top Dog: The Science of Winning and Losing*. Hanin postulated that everyone has an individual zone of optimal functioning: 'This is a level of anxiousness that is beneficial to their performance. Some players need more anxiety to be at their best, others need less. Great performances are logged at almost every level of anxiety. The goal is not to calm competitors to the point of being relaxed, but rather to help them find their optimal zone.'

In our England changing room before a match, there would be areas where no words were spoken, and yet just yards away, players would be listening to music and talking nonsense. These were top players who required very different levels of arousal and anxiety, and they knew that they needed to be close to players who had a similar approach. There is no right or wrong way, though there clearly is a right way to respect your teammates' individual approaches. I learned early on not to go anywhere near Martin Johnson before a Test match with a 'knock knock' joke.

The great coaches and captains understand the importance of difference and individuality within their teams. They allow their players to be the best version of themselves by giving them the autonomy to prepare in their own way, creating fire in the belly and ice in the brain.

World-Class Decision-Making: Highlights

1. Create a compass for decision-making: once you have your magnetic north, you know the direction every decision should point towards.

2. Cut the bureaucracy and reduce the number of stakeholders if you want truer, faster decisions.

3. Use the 40–70 rule: good decisions often demand speed, but not too much. Make sure you have just enough data to make the best possible call.

4. Experience is a powerful resource, but the past is often a poor predictor for the future – the context can change and you might need to change your approach with it.

5. Surround yourself with different perspectives and listen to dissenting voices.

6. Find a way to generate fire in your belly and ice in your brain, in order that you can make good decisions under pressure.

7. Smart leaders and teams don't fear failure, but they do mitigate its consequences and costs.

5. Generosity

'In a team packed with difference, generosity is
often the most precious commodity. Celebrating
your own difference is only part of the job –
you have to embrace everybody else's, too.'

DIFFERENCE   TOGETHERNESS   GROWTH

Rob Henderson is a larger-than-life character who became a kind of cult hero on the British and Irish Lions tour to Australia in 2001. A Lions tour requires selflessness and generosity – these qualities offer the only way you can possibly win. From the moment you meet, you have to give your time, energy and body to the cause. To get the best out of each other, you have to keep offering yourself, both on and off the field.

The Lions historically play two games a week: the Test side plays on Saturday and the hopefuls play on Wednesday. On a good tour, there will be enough movement between the two sides for the hopefuls to believe that a Test call-up is possible. And this happens again and again, because Lions tours never go to plan, thanks to injuries, players finding or losing form and changes in strategy. It was expected that Hendo would play in the midweek team, as he would be a great man to lead the Wednesday side, on and off the pitch.

Hendo certainly led the team *off* the pitch, and he was both the best and the worst roommate ever. I liked alarm calls, cups of hot chocolate and a nicely kept bathroom; Hendo enjoyed the craic. I liked my sleep; Hendo not so much. I would be fast asleep when the lights would go on, with Hendo stepping out on to the balcony for a cigarette as he ordered room service.

Hendo was always keen for a game of cribbage. I love cribbage, and he knew that, so a late-night game of crib would ensue before his batteries finally ran out. What a great man. He trained hard and, while he suspected the pecking order meant that he was unlikely to be first choice, he made light of it and created songs for the team, keeping spirits sky-high. And then, slowly but surely, players fell apart, as they do on gruelling Lions tours. Mike Catt got hurt early and left the tour, and then, the week before the first Test, my Lions injury curse struck again.

In 1997, on the Lions tour of South Africa, I suffered a frightening concussion in the unofficial fourth Test against Orange Free State. The team doctor James Robson thought I was going to die on the pitch – we don't watch that video too often in the Greenwood household, I can tell you. Now, four years later in Australia, I had snapped all my ankle ligaments. I stayed on the tour, desperately trying to recover. I was so close. My ankle gave way a few days before the third and final Test and I could play no part in it.

My loss was Hendo's gain, however, and he barrelled his way into the Test team. The Lions destroyed Australia in the first Test in Brisbane, 'Waltzing O'Driscoll' ringing out among a sea of red. The lads said it had felt like a home game. Melbourne for the second Test saw a reversal of fortunes: the game looked under control for the Lions, but a Richard Hill injury and a Joe Roff intercept try changed everything. In the third Test in Sydney, Daniel Herbert scored two, Justin Harrison stole a lineout to prevent a match-winning Lions try at the death and one of life's great opportunities passed the squad by. It really was the one that got away.

In the changing room after the game there was an air of despondency. I was sitting with Hendo, who did something that will always live with me. He grabbed his Lions Test jersey – number 12 – and gave it to me. 'Shaggy, this should have been yours,' he said. 'I want you to have it.' It was an extraordinary gesture, and I thanked him profusely – but I swore to myself that one day I would return the jersey to its rightful owner.

Some years later, Hendo had a testimonial lunch in London. Around 500 people were rammed into a ballroom to salute the great man. I wasn't due to attend, but I knew I had to get there with my special package. Unannounced, I slipped through the back door, found the MC and asked to have the stage for five minutes at the end of the auction. When I addressed the crowd I told them all the story and we auctioned the shirt, raising £10,000 for Rob's chosen charities. The shirt had delivered again. One act of generosity had led to another, and then 10,000 more.

A CULTURE OF GENEROSITY NEEDS TO BE CURATED

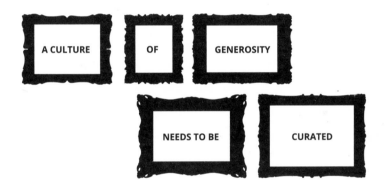

In business, generosity of spirit is no less important, and a team that is dysfunctional will often be lacking this simple ingredient. Competition among the top team is often born from the fact that one executive does not want to see another succeed.

A good leader, on the other hand, will create the structure, culture and incentives to encourage generosity and teamship. They will try to hardwire the concept of shared success and failure into the team, connecting and aligning the deliverables and targets of each person. This isn't easy – human beings are naturally competitive and the corporate world can often create a dynamic where executives are competing with each other for resources, profile and a share of a finite bonus pot. Behaviours such as collaboration and generosity of spirit don't always emerge organically.

How to be a good teammate is one of the first skills that we learn in the workplace. Before we lead direct reports or teams, we only have peer-to-peer relationships. Over time, we tend to focus more on leadership, and we can neglect our teamship skills. The teams that exist at the top of organisations can be nonchalant about each other's success, and sometimes outright competitive. As ever, the tone is set at the top. If the executive team role-models collaborative and generous behaviours, those behaviours will be mirrored further down the organisation. The opposite will also be true, of course.

As a member of the 'top team', it's easy to put positive energy into the team that you lead rather than the executive committee that you are a part of. These individuals will often be such established and capable leaders that they are uncomfortable in any role other than leader. They might have forgotten how to be a good teammate.

Dave Lewis, formerly of Tesco, is incredibly lucid on this topic:

> You need to incentivise good teamplay. People need to be rewarded for each other's success. You need structure and design to facilitate the behaviours that you want. In large organisations, you tend to get recognition and progress for performance in your own area. Then, what can happen when you get to the top of the organisation is that you become the shop steward for your team and area. One of the rules I have for every board that I run is that when you sit at the top table, you must think and act as part of that team. The top team. You must get out of your lane and then lead

your team against the agenda and decisions that we have made together. Some leaders actively create competition; they want 'a pack of wolves' fighting over the meat, but that just drives siloed behaviour and dysfunction.

A good incentive scheme alone cannot create a culture of generosity and collaboration, but it can definitely help. In 2010 Ben created a bespoke bonus scheme for the extended leadership team at BBH. It was called 20-20 and involved the top 20 leaders playing for a bonus pool of 20 per cent of their salary, with each of them scored according to three key metrics:

1. Performance of the business: without hitting the plan, there was no bonus.
2. Performance of the team: some shared goals and shared reward.
3. Performance of the individual: some clear individual deliverables within the team.

The scheme was transparent, quantitative and strategic. Each measure was equally weighted, so Ben was sending a clear signal about the behaviours he wanted to see. He was incentivising good teamship, and the impact was immediate: collaboration went up, competition was reduced and BBH began an extraordinary period of growth.

IT'S YOUR TEAM'S NAME ON THE FRONT OF THE SHIRT AND YOUR NAME ON THE BACK

In many sports, the name of the team is on the front of the shirt and the name of the individual is on the back. I like the signal that sends: the idea that the team comes first and no individual is more important than the team.

No sport exhibits this sense of generosity quite as powerfully as road cycling. In the Tour de France, a team employs a variety of riders in their attempt to put their leader on the podium. There will be specialist sprinters and climbers in each team, but the embodiment of the sport's philosophy of selfless generosity is the domestique. The domestiques are the riders who are there not to win the race but to support the leader. They carry water to them, they let them sit on their wheel to conserve energy and they protect them from the dangers and challenges that the road has in store.

Geraint Thomas is a two-time Olympic gold medallist in track cycling for Team GB, and the winner of the 2018 Tour de France. He has been both a domestique and a leader in his professional cycling career and told me about the inner dynamics of a Tour de France team:

Before turning professional, you are all talented individuals in our own right. And if you're good enough to turn professional, your role suddenly goes from winning races to helping your teammate succeed. You can spend your whole career working for others – it's the way the sport works. There's no way anyone could win the Tour de France without a strong team around them. Since turning professional in 2007, I've had many years playing this support role. As a support rider, the key for me was to find my own successes within the race. Each year, I wanted my role in the team to come later and later into the race, closer and closer to the finish. Instead of finishing my job with two climbs to go, I wanted to make it to the final climb, or the final five kilometres, or get to the finish with my leader. I wanted to be my leader's right-hand man. And even though it wouldn't be me stood on the podium, I would know that my leader wouldn't have been there without my help. It gave me a buzz and immense satisfaction. I've been with Chris Froome for all four of his Tour de France wins, and I know I played my part in all of them. Within the peloton and the cycling community, you earn great respect by being a 'super-domestique' or main helper, and it's a job you're proud to do. It can even pay well, but that recognition doesn't filter into the wider community. It's certainly not the job for you if you're in it for the headlines.

I've been lucky enough to have a team supporting and riding 100 per cent in my 'service'. To have seven or eight other guys fully committed to helping me win is an amazing feeling. You can dig a little deeper in the final stages of the race knowing the boys have given you everything.

When he stood on the top step of the podium in Paris in 2018, proudly wearing his yellow jersey, Geraint Thomas knew that he was there in no small part thanks to the hard work and dedication of his teammates.

It's a core philosophy shared by elite levels of the military, as special forces veteran Jason Fox explained when he told me about the supposedly 'softer' skills of leadership: 'SAS selection is a nine-month interview. It comes down to a simple question for the selection panel: in a ditch under fire, do I want that guy next to me? You'll see some of the strongest and fittest candidates not make it, because when it comes to characteristics like trust, loyalty and compassion, they fall short – they just haven't got that humanity about them that makes all the difference.'

These aren't the words of an HR director; this is a top operator from the finest fighting force on the planet. Being elite doesn't mean that you can't be compassionate; in fact, the special forces believe that you have to be in order to thrive.

THERE IS A SPECIAL TYPE OF PLAYER WHO MAKES EVERY OTHER PLAYER BETTER

Richard Hill has 71 England caps and 13 tries to his name, in addition to three British and Irish Lions tours. Those numbers don't even begin to tell the full story – sometimes you have to play with someone to understand how good they are. Ask the average man in the street for the key names in our 2003 England side and I wager that Hilly would be mentioned pretty late on. But if you asked the players, I guarantee that he would come near the top of everyone's list.

Richard Hill was so important to our team that he made Sir Clive break one of his golden rules. We had learned the cost of carrying an injured player in your squad when we blew the Grand Slam 2001, after which Clive decided that no individual was worth that risk – it would put more workload on all the other players and they might break down, too. But when Richard Hill pulled his hamstring in the first match of the 2003 World Cup, there was no return plane ticket booked for him. He was deemed too important to our side and a subclause was added to our team rules in order to accommodate the great man.

Hilly stayed with us and did not play or train for four weeks. When he returned for the semi-final five weeks later and went straight into the team, no one questioned it. If Richard Hill was fit, he played.

When game day came, he was always relaxed but focused, and he did what needed to be done. He cleaned up messes, covered holes and linked the ball to space; he downed monster men in the narrow channels and hunted down flyers in the open spaces. He was truly extraordinary at the ordinary. His basics were world class. He wasn't the strongest or the quickest, but when you have a man who never errs, it allows others to flourish.

Hilly didn't care about headlines. He led a simple life away from the floodlights and big match stadia. He gave everything he had to every team he ever played for and it cost him dearly physically, as he finished his career carrying a multitude of injuries.

As Eddie Jones's team manager, Hilly is now giving the current crop of England players the same spirit of generosity that he gave to all of us. He's an elegant point of connection between our two teams, and there's no better man to represent the class of 2003.

I recently interviewed Sale Sharks teammates and twin brothers Tom and Ben Curry on my podcast and asked them which back row player from the past they would most like to play with. To my delight, Tom chose Hilly.

In a team packed with differences, sometimes one of them is the ability to lift your teammates' performance. There are some players who consistently bring the best out of their partners, but they can be hard to identify when the value of their work is packaged in the feats of their teammates rather than their own. They are the domestiques. Why did I rate the Welsh centre Allan Bateman so highly? Because he got the very best out of me. He knew when to give me a space and how to put me into it, but also when I needed his support and strength. In attack and defence, he was a giant. We played together on the Lions tour in 1997. Unless you played with him, you probably didn't know how good he was – he was a player's player.

At BBH, Ben worked with Jon Peppiatt, an executive at the top of the agency. Jon's entire working focus was on helping make his partners better. He cleared the path and mopped up afterwards. He knew when to build people up and when to bring them down a peg or two. Despite a modest academic career, he was the most emotionally intelligent person in any team he was in. He always knew what to say and who to say it to, and rarely used the big platforms to drive his agenda. He preferred a quiet word or a gentle arm around the shoulder. When asked to talk about leadership to a group of senior BBH-ers, he titled his speech 'Leading from the Back'. Pep's generosity of spirit made him a critical member of a highly successful team. He wasn't often the guy winning the pitches or creating the work, but he was always busy in the background, supporting and protecting the team. This type of executive asks themselves different questions to the ones that most people ask. How can I best serve the team? What do my teammates need from me? How can I put them in front of goal so that they can score? These people clear the path; they facilitate and smooth over. Their best work might happen in one on ones rather than on the big stages and set pieces. If you don't have this archetype in your team, you should try to find one – they will help you to go further, and they will get you there faster.

EVERY TEAM NEEDS SOMEONE
WHO CAN SET THE RHYTHM

Sir Steve Redgrave and Matthew Pinsent had won gold in the coxless pair in the 1992 Olympics in Barcelona and again at Atlanta four years later. For the 2000 Olympics in Sydney, they switched to the coxless four. The four men who made up the crew were all supreme athletes, but they were all very different. Redgrave was the strongest and most powerful. Pinsent had the lungs of a horse and was fastest over the Olympic distance of 2,000 metres, whereas James Cracknell was the quickest over 5,000 metres or more. Tim Foster was the fourth member of the crew, and for the purposes of this chapter, the most intriguing. He was not the best at any of the physical tests the four did, nor was he the biggest or most powerful, and yet James Cracknell is clear that they wouldn't have won gold without him:

Conventional thinking would have been to have Matt Pinsent and Steve Redgrave, the Olympic Champions in the coxless pair, guys who knew each other's rowing so well, in the stern of the boat, where the rhythm is set and then tack Tim and myself into the boat behind them. We tried that and it just didn't work – the idiosyncrasies developed by Steve and Matt over the years meant that the boat felt like two pairs rather than one four. We had to split Steve and Matt up, but the problem was that for the last decade, they'd only ever rowed with each other. This meant that someone sitting between them had to bring out the best in them but not compromise his rowing in the process. That required someone who was supremely confident in their technique, metronomically consistent, very relaxed but wouldn't compromise his rowing to make the boat comfortable. That summed up Tim perfectly. He knew exactly how he wanted to row, knew he couldn't match Steve, Matt or me for power, but knew also that we couldn't win without him. Tim was relentless in his quest for the most efficient rhythm. His theory was that if he created that rhythm and platform, the three of us could unleash our power.

They say that any truly great band needs a truly great drummer, and Tim Foster played that role for this team. In setting the rhythm and keeping the beat he got the best out of his teammates, winning Olympic gold in the process.

Who sets the tone and the rhythm for your team? Who makes people feel good and might be contributing more than their numbers suggest? We tend to value most highly the things that we can measure most precisely, and yet not every contribution is tangible. The culture of a team or business can be all-powerful, yet it's often very hard to quantify. Cultural contribution can sometimes be seen as a soft contribution, yet if you interpret culture to be how you behave and make people feel, it is of paramount importance.

A GENEROUS LEADER ABSORBS PRESSURE AND PROTECTS THEIR TEAM

Martin Johnson wouldn't ask you to do anything he wasn't willing to do himself. We used to joke that if he asked you to run through a brick wall, you would. Why? Because there'd be a giant Johnno-shaped hole where he'd already been through it.

Johnson's rugby intelligence was off the charts. He had a little more pace than anyone gave him credit for, and soft, skilful hands. But he knew that his role in the team was to put his head and body in places that no intelligent person would ever contemplate. He was our leader, our enforcer and, on occasion, our protector.

Once the number four was on his back, he limited any desire to play in the wider channels and focused on policing the heavy traffic. In a world where it seems we want everyone to be all things to all people, Martin understood his super-strengths and focused relentlessly on honing and delivering them.

In the World Cup semi-final in 2003, we were playing France. Serge Betsen scored first, and the rain was coming down. It was a brutally physical Test match – it always is against the French. I made a tackle, and fell to the floor on the French side of the ball, at the mercy of their arriving forwards. The laws now say you can't 'ruck', the act of removing someone from near the ball using your boots. The use of television match officials and law changes in modern rugby means your safety is almost guaranteed; you are not likely to have the shirt removed from your back as forwards spot the opportunity to rough up a three-quarter back who has lost his way.

But that is now, and this was then. I knew what was coming, and I knew it would hurt. I assumed the foetal position, closed my eyes and waited, but nothing happened. I waited a little longer, and still no French boots were using me as a doormat. I dared to open one eye, and then the second. Looming large and straddling over me, his giant arms outstretched, was Martin Osborne Johnson – heroic times call for his full name. Martin had one French shirt in his outstretched right hand and another in his left, while he used his forehead to butt away anyone else in a blue shirt who wanted to have a go at me. He looked down at me and said, 'Shaggy, what are you doing in here? Get out there and find us some space.' I didn't need asking twice. Like a rat up a drainpipe, I was gone.

This is what all great leaders do. They absorb pressure, shield you from incoming challenges and give you the 'air cover' you need to perform, develop and grow. There is nothing more empowering than knowing that your boss has your back, allowing you to focus on the delivery of your job. These kind of bosses won't all look like Johnno, but they will share his spirit.

BE GENEROUS TO YOURSELF

Victoria Milligan is a motivational speaker who endured the most horrific tragedy while on a family break in Cornwall in 2013. Her husband and daughter were killed in a boating accident, while she lost a leg and her son sustained terrible injuries. Her reflections about grief, bereavement and finding the strength to carry on are as upsetting as they are inspirational.

One of the lessons that she shares involves the inner monologue that we all carry around with us. During her darkest moments, she felt almost envious of her beloved husband Nick for dying and being spared the pain that she was suffering. She was scared of facing her grief, and when her thoughts turned to herself, she was critical to the point of cruelty. At that moment, she explains, she was given a powerful piece of advice: 'Try to speak to yourself the way you would speak to your closest friend.'

This involves being kind to yourself, being as loving, caring and generous as you would be to your nearest and dearest. Sometimes, it's an achievement just to get through the week. In those circumstances, it's not helpful to be too self-critical of your own performance. Sometimes, you've just got to get your head down and keep going.

We will return to this idea in our chapter on wellbeing, but for now it is worth holding on to the idea that we should all try to be our own biggest champion rather than our harshest critic – heaven knows there are enough of those around.

I want to close this chapter by sharing an extraordinary moment that took place during my interview with the Curry twins. Ben Curry had been due to be the first of the brothers to represent England, against the Barbarians in 2018, but a back spasm meant that he was replaced by his brother. Tom went on to be man of the match in that game and hasn't looked back, while Ben has not been picked for England since. I asked Ben how it had felt to watch his twin play in a World Cup final, and whether, as well as pride, there wasn't also an ounce of 'that could have been me'.

Ben's reply was a masterclass in generosity. 'I never thought it could have been me, because that discredits Tom a lot,' said Ben. 'He won man of the match on his debut. He then had two years where he played very well, and he then got man of the match in the quarter-final. I have a huge amount of work to do to get to where he is.'

That's brotherhood, and that's generosity. And with that kind of attitude, I'm sure that Ben's time will come.

World-Class Generosity: Highlights

1. In a team packed with difference, generosity can be your most precious commodity.

2. Being generous not only pays back, but it also makes you feel good.

3. Encourage, incentivise and set an example if you want a culture of generosity to flourish.

4. Find your Richard Hill. It's a special kind of person that makes their colleagues better, and it's not always an easy skill to spot.

5. Sometimes being generous as a leader means taking one for the team.

6. Be generous with yourself: sometimes, just getting through the week is a win.

7. Just as every great band has a great drummer, every great team needs someone to set the rhythm.

PART II

FORGING
TOGETHERNESS

6. Purpose

'The strategy and tactics will evolve, but the purpose should be more of a constant, not to be changed lightly. Like the North Star, it should be a guiding light and a compass for decision-making.'

DIFFERENCE | TOGETHERNESS | GROWTH

There are times in my past when I wish I'd scribbled down the details of what I would later realise were life-changing moments. One such occasion was the meeting in which Sir Clive Woodward told us that he really didn't care too much about beating Wales, Scotland, Ireland and France. Those are nice games to win, he explained, but they are not the big prize. Winning and losing games against those teams would be 'gateways' to a much more ambitious destination: World Cup glory.

The only teams who had won the Webb Ellis Trophy before 2003 were the big three: the southern hemisphere giants, New Zealand, Australia and South Africa. And 18 years on, they are still the only teams other than England to have won a World Cup. Getting to number one in the world by beating those guys regularly was the mission. If we could do that, we would be ready to win the Rugby World Cup. Sir Clive's words didn't land with everyone, but they lit a fire in a core group of players. He had defined our new purpose.

If task one for any leader is to pack their team with difference, task two is to create a sense of togetherness. In this part, we will explore how elite teams and progressive businesses forge togetherness. How they leverage their past to help define their future, use their culture and communication as strategic amplifiers, create structures and reward schemes to incentivise the behaviours that they want to see from their executives and, finally, how they build teamship and encourage generosity as a key leadership behaviour. To forge is to apply heat and pressure in order to make something stronger. Just as steel will become sharper, more flexible and more resilient after it has been forged, so will a team.

The journey towards forging true togetherness begins with purpose. A good purpose answers the question 'Why are we here?' It is not the goal – it is the reason. A reason for getting out of bed in the morning, something that makes your company unique and your endeavours worthwhile. Your purpose should connect with you emotionally as well as rationally; connect the organisation's past with its future; and connect employees at every level and in every department.

A good purpose should make team members and employees feel proud; it should create context for the more mundane parts of the job and elevate daily actions to a more rewarding plane. A strong purpose connects the belief system of the employee to the values of the organisation, creating a shared sense of identity, belonging and togetherness.

A good purpose will act as a compass for decision-making. 'The purpose needs to help you to answer the question when nobody else is in the room,' says Dave Lewis of Tesco. 'One of the things that I'm quietly proudest of about my time at Tesco is that during the Covid-19 crisis, nobody really asked for permission. So all those years of saying that the purpose was our magnetic north, and that if you make a decision with the purpose in mind then it will be the right decision, really paid off. In this crisis, that was tested. Our people just got on and did the right thing. It was something to behold.'

There is always a much greater chance of a purpose landing if the team has created it together, if emotional ownership of these binding ideas is shared and the team responsible for creating the plan is also the team responsible for delivering it. A purpose that is simply handed down from above will never be as powerful.

Your purpose must have ambition, but it must also be credible. It should be fixed and unmoving. The strategy and tactics will evolve, but the purpose should be a constant, not to be changed lightly. A great purpose will connect the individual with the team, and it will connect your short- and long-term goals.

In the business world, few companies have committed to purpose as meaningfully as Unilever. Former CEO Paul Polman spent a decade putting a purposeful agenda at the heart of the company's business strategy, before Alan Jope, with whom we spoke for this book, took over at the start of 2019. Unilever operates in 190 countries, employing 150,000 people, and in 2019 they delivered 51 billion euros of revenue.

'At Unilever, we have three core beliefs that sit at the heart of everything that we do,' says Alan. 'We believe that brands with purpose grow, that companies with purpose last and that people with purpose thrive.'

For Alan, this agenda is at the centre of his leadership beliefs. When he took over at Unilever, he and his team articulated the following priorities: 'To manage the world's finest portfolio of purposeful brands. To prove the relationship between purpose and performance. To be a beacon for diversity and inclusion.'

So, let's explore what makes a good purpose, the difference between purpose and mission, and how elite cultures give their purpose daily application and utility. We'll begin by looking at how we might use purpose to connect the present with the future.

YOUR PURPOSE SHOULD CONNECT YOUR
SHORT- AND LONG-TERM GOALS

Under Ben's watch, BBH's purpose was refined in 2016. BBH had ten beliefs, crafted in the 1980s by the three co-founders, John Bartle, Sir Nigel Bogle and Sir John Hegarty. They were displayed proudly in every BBH office around the world.

Ben and his team began a process of trying to distil these ten beliefs down to a single sentence. They knew that difference was going to be central – the black sheep is BBH's logo and ideological symbol – but they also wanted to capture the idea of using creativity for good. After many months of not quite finding the right expression, a dinner was fixed between co-founder Sir Nigel Bogle and Brian Bacon, founder of Oxford Leadership and a purpose and growth guru, to help BBH with the distillation process.

After an evening spent talking about difference, the black sheep and the past and future of BBH, Sir Nigel took the short walk from an Italian restaurant in Barnes back to his home. Just outside a branch of Londis, a sentence popped into his head: 'The power of difference to make a difference.'

Nigel phoned it through to Ben, and they both knew immediately that he had cracked it. The new purpose reasserted the business's fundamental commitment to creativity. It spoke to the impact and effectiveness of that creativity for clients, but it also touched upon the power of difference to impact the lives of people within BBH and beyond – not bad for eight words. Given that the line had been coined by one of the co-founders, it had the authority and credibility needed to stick.

The impact of this evolved purpose was immediate. People began asking each other two questions: 'Is this creative work different enough?' and 'Will this work really make a difference?' When your purpose becomes a question, you know that it's starting to live within the organisation. In 2018, BBH won the IPA Effectiveness Awards Grand Prix and was crowned the Company of the Year. These highly coveted awards are awarded for the commercial effectiveness and return on investment of campaigns, so they were an important validation of the new purpose. BBH went on to win agency of the year and the Grand Prix again in 2020 – the team is clearly still using 'the power of difference to make a difference'.

If the mission is your 'what', the purpose should be your 'why'. It should elevate daily activity and action to a higher plane. It should connect your short- and longer-term goals because people need to understand the context in which they are operating. If they are going to operate at high levels of intensity and endeavour for extended periods, they need an inspiring goal. Mapping out this destination in a way that feels vivid, energising and real is the task of the leader. One of my favourite definitions of leadership is that 'a leader takes you to places that you wouldn't go to by yourself'.

With the destination set, the task is then to break down the journey into tangible short-term sections. A battle may be lost along the way, but if it is framed within the broader purpose, a setback will not be fatal and the war can still be won. There is international competition on the way to an Olympics, and there is a Six Nations every year of a Rugby World Cup cycle. These are short-term obstacles and opportunities that can be used to build towards the long-term goal.

'ME, WE'

'Me, We' might be the shortest poem in the English language. It was delivered by Muhammad Ali at the Harvard graduation address in 1975, and the more I reflect on it, the more profound and brilliant I think it is. In the space of just two words, the legendary boxer asks two of the biggest questions in life: who am I? And who are we?

Me: What are my values, how will I carry myself and what do I want my life's work to be?

We: Who is my partner, who are my friends and what tribe do I want to be part of?

'Me, We' is the essence of leadership and teamship. It connects the individual with the team and organisation. It says that we are all part of something bigger: a family, a team, a company, a community. Being a purposeful individual or organisation means acknowledging that you are accountable to others and that your behaviours have an impact.

'We can now prove that people who can connect their personal purpose with the purpose of the organisation will be more resilient, more energised and more productive,' says Alan Jope. 'If there is no overlap between your personal purpose and the work that you do, you'll collapse – you just won't have the reserves of energy needed to keep going.'

Dan Carter, the New Zealand rugby legend, talks about the fact that every All Black is driven by the desire to 'hand the shirt on bigger and better than you found it'. Core to this is the idea that the individual only ever has the national shirt on loan. You are one person in a line stretching back to the nineteenth century, and onwards into the future. Your task is to wear the shirt with pride and invest it with even greater meaning so that when you hand it on to the next guy in line, it is even better.

The essence of any successful team lies in a shared identity and sense of purpose. It is the leader's job to create the connections necessary to foster a sense of tribe. What values do we share? How do we want to behave? What will be our goals, and what kind of legacy do we want to leave behind? These are not easy questions to answer. They require time spent together and a level of candour that is not often found in the workplace, which is why getting a team 'off-site' or stimulating this kind of discussion with an exercise or challenge can be so helpful.

Ben has learned over many years that purpose is a tough nut to crack if you're just staring at a blank piece of paper. It's much more productive to invite a senior team to talk about their individual beliefs, and then to bridge those values to the organisation's reason for being. This process can't be rushed. It requires a diverse group of people and a diverse set of inputs. The key is to keep asking good questions, until the purpose reveals itself. Questions like:

- What are the beliefs and values that connect our past and our future?
- How do our products and services make a difference to the lives of our customers?
- Why does what we do matter?

They say that a good process often has 'a beginning, a muddle and an end', and the muddle is the tough bit. Don't give up and keep pushing through, because you'll know when you've got to something that's good enough.

Of course, agreeing the purpose is only the first part of the job. It then needs to be launched, embedded and activated, a process that requires time, effort and expertise. Too often, the steering group falls short at this critical stage of the process – just when the purpose needs to be embedded and role-modelled, the leadership's focus moves on. For every minute spent working on the purpose, you should spend ten minutes activating it. We'll discuss how to communicate the purpose in more detail in Chapter 9.

SIMPLE, STICKY AND REALISTIC

Special coaches have the gift of brevity. They know how to say a great deal without saying much at all. According to

George Armitage Miller, one of the founders of cognitive psychology, the average human can hold seven, 'plus or minus two', items in their head at one time. Imagine your normal working day. How many thoughts are flying around your brain? The worries, the to-do lists, the general buzz of activity. Then imagine the stress of an international sports fixture and throw in a heart rate of 200 and an aching shoulder. Your coach has to keep it simple.

Ben Hunt-Davis is a former British rower who won a gold medal in the men's eight at the Sydney Olympics in 2000. He has written a book that explores the seven-word question that came to drive all of their decisions as a squad: *Will It Make the Boat Go Faster?*

'For the GB men's rowing eight in the two years leading up to the Sydney 2000 Olympics,' Ben says, 'our mission, or what was most important to us, was very, very clear: to win the Olympic gold medal. We knew that we couldn't control whether we won because we couldn't control how fast the opposition was, so we started asking the question "Will it make the boat go faster?" before we did anything. Every conversation or discussion, every decision, every action: was it going to make the boat go faster? It led to us changing our training centre, the equipment we used, our decision-making process, our briefing and performance reviews, how we interacted as a group. We challenged everything, based on what we had all agreed was most important.'

By turning your purpose into a question, you can turn a four-year mission into a compass for daily decision-making. Every choice is suddenly filtered through this simple lens.

In business, we often let things get unnecessarily complicated. They say that 'simplicity is the ultimate sophistication', and yet corporate missions and purposes often lack the brutal simplicity that we see in the military or in sport.

As we went into extra time in the World Cup final in 2003, the messages got simpler. Sir Clive ran down to Wilko to share a simple piece of 'tactical genius': 'Kick, kick, kick.' He says now it's the only time Wilko ever swore at him. Martin Johnson's message was almost as simple: 'If you see a bloke in yellow with the ball, smack him. If you have the ball, go forward. Don't leave this field a beaten man.' Then he legged it, preparing himself for his job as a player. A giant man with a giant number four on the back of his jersey, he knew what needed to be done – and so did we.

People who have the gift of brevity are hugely valuable in the workplace – it takes a special type of intelligence to distil an issue down to its core essence. We all know people who start talking and decide what they are going to say as they go. We might also know people who 'talk least and talk last', and the latter group tends to be worth listening to.

Of course, your purpose can be as simple and sticky as you like, but if it's not realistic, it's going to come undone pretty quickly. Think of it as being like a piece of elastic: you can stretch it so far, until a point at which it snaps. I wonder if Eddie Jones went too far with his announcement in 2019 that he wanted England to become 'the greatest team that ever played'. His declaration was certainly simple and sticky – but for all the wrong reasons, as it preceded an embarrassing loss in Paris. History is littered with quotes that should have stayed within the team room. By all means aim high, but it's a good idea to make sure you're the best team in the world before you worry about being the best team ever.

YOUR PURPOSE CAN HELP WITH SELECTION

With the purpose defined, it becomes easier to select players or employees who buy into your values and mission. At interview, the purpose is often a great thing to talk about. It will elevate a conversation beyond the traditional and often tiresome CV run-through. It will flush out whether your 'why' really resonates with the individual.

Sir Dave Brailsford is the coach who led the British cycling team to the top of the medal table at the 2008 and 2012 Olympics, and, as manager of Team Sky (now Team Ineos), he oversaw a long line of Tour de France successes. He has this to say about selection:

So, apart from talent and form, what else are we looking for when we select any team line-up? First off, hunger. The passion to win. It's always a hunger game and previous success should only enhance rather than diminish the desire for more.

Second, sacrifice. Every member needs to put the needs of the team above their own and to do whatever it takes to help win. Every rider needs to endure real physical pain and suffering for the greater good.

Third, character. Every team needs strong characters who can look after themselves and, crucially, look after each other. The Tour de France is a hot-house, high-pressure environment, a great travelling circus with millions of people on the road, where every slip-up is magnified and analysed by the global media. You have to have the mental strength to thrive in that goldfish bowl, and it's not for everyone. Character means the ability to respond in the moment to pressure. No sporting competition, at any level, runs in straight lines. Three years ago [in 2017], Chris Froome won the Tour by under a minute, after a number of challenging mechanical issues on the road. If his teammates hadn't reacted instantly and made the right judgements for him in the very moment they happened, he would have lost. They are the margins between success and failure.

Hunger, sacrifice and character. Brailsford knows exactly what he's looking for, because he knows exactly what his team's purpose is. And it works both ways: a strong and clear purpose appeals to the best talent.

As we stated at the beginning of this chapter, Unilever has proved emphatically that purpose pays, and one pillar of their agenda is sustainability. The business case is impressive. 'We have 28 sustainable living brands,' says Alan Jope. 'They now constitute 60 per cent of our revenues, and they are growing 60 per cent faster than the rest of the portfolio. There have been cost savings of over 800 million euros from our more sustainable resourcing, essentially from using less. The great myth is that sustainability adds cost, when in fact it takes costs away.

'We have also learned that our sustainability strategy is an absolute magnet for the top talent. We recruit graduate trainees in 54 markets around the world; in 52 of those, we are the number one employer in our sector of choice. We also know that 90 per cent of the 150,000 people who work for us say that they are proud to work for Unilever.'

This sentiment is echoed in a very different kind of business. As Rich Pierson of Headspace says, 'When you are a purpose-driven company, you attract a lot of people who are very purpose-driven. They hold you to very high standards. If you fall short, you get called out on it.'

Above and beyond the many reasons that purpose matters is the simple truth that pride among employees drives loyalty and performance. It shouldn't be a choice between profit or purpose; you should view purpose as a pathway to better profits.

WHY BEFORE WHAT AND HOW

A purpose is your North Star, and it should not be changed lightly. A good leader will not change the purpose for the sake of it. They will embrace an existing purpose if it provides clarity, meaning and empowerment, but if it is falling short on any of these criteria, it must be changed. If you are going to evolve the purpose of the business, be sure to do so for the right reasons and at the right time. Make sure that you have enough data to make an informed decision, that you've spoken to enough people and that you've heard from all parts of the business.

Carolyn McCall is the CEO of ITV. As CEO of easyJet, she oversaw record passenger numbers and profits and the airline's entry into the FTSE 100. 'Defining the purpose tends to be one of the earlier things I get to,' she says, 'but I don't think it should be too early. You have to meet a lot of people and learn the business first. That can take a few months if you're an external appointment. If you find during that period that people aren't clear enough about the purpose, about their "why", then you need to relook at it.

'When I got to easyJet in 2010, the DNA was there, but we needed to align everyone and remind people about what we were founded to do. We rewrote the purpose to: "Make travel easy and affordable." That purpose drove everything that we did. It was simple, it was memorable and it resonated with every role in the airline. It came from the DNA of the company. "Easy" led to allocated seating, the easy-to-use app, no scrums at the gate. But it all had to be delivered in an "affordable" way, and so that drove our low-cost model. The mission before we got to that purpose was a jumble of words that nobody could remember. When landing the purpose, the way you communicate is so important. Leaders can forget that communicating is as much about listening as talking. You can't land a purpose by just talking about it. Your actions and how you listen and respond really matter.'

If you can evolve your purpose through crafting, embedding and activating it in a really committed fashion, you can create very high levels of empowerment and agility within your organisation. People will not need to ask for permission, because they will know that they are exercising freedom within a framework. Rulebooks rarely work, but if you can be really tight on a few strategic principles, you can be really flexible on the executional practices. Top talent wants freedom to operate. So be clear on your strategic intent, and then unleash your talent in a way that's accountable.

An inspiring new purpose will connect the short and long term in the same way that it will connect the individual and the team. Too often, the purpose is a piece of thinking or writing that lives more in words than in deeds. When activating and embedding a new purpose, the task is to bring it off the page and make it live within the organisation.

A good purpose will make you feel as well as think, speaking to the heart as well as the head. In that famous 'reset' meeting at the start of my England career, the memory of how Sir Clive made me feel is much more vivid than his exact words. It gives me goose bumps to recall it now – he had lit a fire in many of us. I remember looking around and knowing that we had a new purpose, a new gold standard, and that nothing would ever be the same again.

World-Class Purpose: Highlights

1. A company's purpose is its 'why' – it's your reason for being, articulated as one simple and sticky expression. Spend time getting it right.

2. A strong purpose draws upon a company's past and looks confidently towards its future.

3. 'Me, We': when the company's purpose aligns with that of the individual, you can create fierce resolve.

4. The purpose must marry your short- and long-term goals, so you never lose sight of the bigger picture.

5. The purpose should be a compass for decision-making, helping you to navigate issues, big and small.

6. A good purpose will be rational and emotional; it will speak to the head and the heart.

7. Creating the purpose is only the beginning: you then need to spend your time really activating it and *living* it.

7. Coaching

'Coaches see things that players can't feel, and players feel things that coaches can't see.'

DIFFERENCE   TOGETHERNESS   GROWTH

We said in the introduction that there is no one chapter on leadership because it runs through the whole book, but this chapter constitutes the closest thing we have. All of the coaches that we will reference here are leaders, not least because they created growth for individuals, teams and organisations. Legendary coaches such as Jürgen Gröbler, Sir Clive Woodward and Sir Dave Brailsford all set a vision, defined a system and a style, and then created a winning environment. Like great CEOs, they surround themselves with specialists and delegate responsibility without ever abdicating it. They understand that athletes need a voice and that a two-way flow of ideas and feedback is critical, but they also let it be known that they are in charge and that no single individual can ever become bigger than the team.

We will use the terms 'coach' and 'leader' interchangeably, but there are a couple of distinctions that are worth making. In sport, the coach never steps onto the field or scores, whereas a business leader may be required to lead by example. It's also worth noting that in business, 'coaching' can mean getting help from an external consultant or expert. Coaching can also refer to a specific leadership style that is less hands-on and more consultative and empowering, a style more reflective of a chairperson than a CEO. It implies that there is a little distance from the action, and some perspective with regard to performance.

In sport, coaches come in many different shapes and sizes. There is the on-field, tracksuit-wearing practitioner, never more comfortable than when he or she is working with athletes. Then there is the coach who operates more like a general, standing on the high ground and surveying their troops. These coaches are confident enough to empower specialist coaches and players to execute the day-to-day tasks of skill development and team tactics.

In Sir Clive Woodward's England team, we spent a good deal of time off the field and in training developing the 'backs moves' – carefully planned and choreographed set plays. Clive would come up with a new move and give it a name. We would then play around with it, but we would always keep Clive's original name. In some cases, the name was the only thing that stayed the same. When it came to game day and we scored, Clive would ask us which move we'd used and we would respond with a name that he recognised. 'Told you that would work,' he'd say with a smile. We would smile too.

To me, this is the very definition of a confident player–coach relationship. A confident coach will throw out an idea and have it stress-tested by the players; a confident player will take a good idea and make it their own.

I've heard it said that a coach will see things a player can't feel, and that a player will feel things that a coach can't see. A confident player–coach relationship is one where learning is high-cadence and two-way; where the on- and off-pitch perspectives are embraced and where there is a degree of positive or managed tension. A coaching idea can look world class on paper and then be found wanting in practice. The same is true in business, when a strategy that looked great in theory falls short in execution, which leads to the million-dollar question: is it our execution that's letting down a robust strategy, or do we have a more fundamental problem? To fully interrogate this question, all parties need to be watching carefully and speaking candidly. Only a group of players and coaches together can figure it out. You need people on the pitch giving their perspective, and people in the dugout giving theirs.

Lawrence Dallaglio has a brilliant expression about the optimal relationship between players and coaches. He believes that the most successful teams are 'coach-led but player-driven'. He explains that a world-class coach will create an environment where they challenge their players, and where their players challenge them back. 'The alchemy is created by the positive pressure between players and coaches.'

The relationship between coach and captain in sport is like that between a chairman and an MD in business. The analogy is not perfect, but it is close enough. There should be shared goals and shared values, but a difference in focus. The coach or chairman requires a sense of perspective and objectivity; they should be looking at the playing field from above, rather than being immersed in the action. The captain or MD will have a different perspective. They should be in the thick of things, seeing and feeling the dynamics of play close-up. High-quality decision-making and selection requires both perspectives, of course.

There will be wins and losses for any coach, but at the most basic level, their focus should be fixed on creating growth for the individual, the team and the organisation.

THE TELESCOPE AND THE MICROSCOPE

In sport and business, there is the big picture to focus on – the long-term aims, the World Cup or Olympics – and the more immediate challenge – the next match, the next working day. And you need a different lens for each.

The big picture requires the telescope: setting the mission and developing a winning philosophy and style. This requires you to paint a picture of an inspiring destination, and to build the capabilities required to get you there.

The microscope is the six inches in front of your face. It's execution, core skills and this week's firefight – reactive initiatives and short-term delivery.

A great coach is as adept with the telescope as they are with the microscope; they can set a long-term purpose and work on short-term delivery. I've observed first-hand that this is a characteristic of many of the great CEOs: they will move from big picture to small detail in a heartbeat, shifting between macro strategy and micro execution without breaking stride.

The reason this is such a superpower is because many executives are able to do one of these two things really well, but the most special talent is able to do both.

Sir Andrew Strauss was England cricket captain when the Test side was the best in the world, with Andy Flower as his coach. He talks insightfully about the challenge faced by all elite coaches: 'No coach can afford too many losses on his CV. They will often be tempted by short-term solutions, but ultimately, no coach will achieve anything truly special if he is unable to stay the course and execute a longer-term strategy. When we went to Australia in 2010, both Andy Flower and I received huge criticism for being too negative in our tactics and not grabbing the game by the scruff of the neck. Ultimately, however, our whole strategy relied on us bowling maidens, building pressure and suffocating the Aussies' scoring to the extent that they would play a rash shot in an attempt to "break out". This was not a strategy to which we could half-commit. Andy had the courage to see it through, despite the noise.'

A good leader or coach will make it absolutely clear what the team is trying to achieve in the short, medium and long term. They will identify the mountain that the team is trying to climb and the key landmarks along the way. Goals will be set and the key metrics for measuring performance will be agreed. Nobody can see the future and the past is often a poor predictor of it, but as leaders, we must try to paint a picture of the future that we want to create.

MANAGEMENT BY MANTRA

We spoke in the last chapter about the ability of great coaches to keep things simple. It's a real gift for any leader or coach in business or sport who is able to distil complex ideas and philosophies into simple, memorable language that lives in the organisation and has day-to-day utility.

Sir Nigel Bogle, one of the three co-founders of BBH, talks about the concept of 'management by mantra'. How, as founders, he, John Bartle and Sir John Hegarty created a number of simple and memorable phrases that became part of the corporate vocabulary. Phrases like 'When the world zigs, zag', 'None of us is as good as all of us' and 'Our objective is effectiveness, our strategy is creativity'. These ideas were passed from generation to generation and became the foundations upon which the culture of BBH was built.

But this simplicity doesn't just have to apply to long-term philosophies baked into a corporate or team culture – it's as relevant to the microscope as it is the telescope. It's something Shaun Edwards, a former rugby league player and current assistant defence coach for the France rugby union team, has found invaluable when facing the language challenges inherent in working

126

with the French side. He is quoted as saying: 'I only need a few phrases for my coaching – I like to keep things simple.'

While there is beauty in brevity, a coach's language must be more than just simple. Scott 'Razor' Robertson, coach of the Crusaders and three-time winner of New Zealand's domestic competition, the Super 14, talks a lot about the importance of creating a consistently positive dialogue with players. 'Keep your eyes up' is different to 'Don't look down'. 'Catch everything' is better than 'Don't drop the ball'. It might sound small, but over time, your choice of language contributes to a culture that looks for opportunities rather than one that fears making mistakes. Scott keeps it simple, and he keeps it positive.

I think this is a brilliant example of using positivity as a filter in everything that you do. Could you find more positive expressions for the points that you want to make? Saying something like 'I know you've got this' rather than 'Don't let me down' could make all the difference. Our language is central to how we make people feel, so give it the time and care it deserves.

THEY ARE CALLED HEAD
COACHES FOR A REASON

HEAD COACHES

Jürgen Gröbler and Sir Alex Ferguson coached very different sports and are very different people, but Sir Matthew Pinsent and Gary Neville talk about them in similar terms.

'Gröbler was the best man manager that I ever met,' says Pinsent of the most successful Olympic coach in British rowing history. 'He could shoehorn huge egos into small boats, season in, season out, and get everyone thinking, training and behaving alike. Very early on in my partnership with Steve, we were dominating the field in the early-season races and getting a bit cocky, even bored, with the challenge. What did he do? He instructed us not to be ahead until halfway in a 2,000 metre race. He imposed a rate cap [a maximum number of strokes per minute], to essentially clip our wings. We were dumbfounded and extremely nervous. Why should you attempt to go slower than you naturally would? We went out and duly were in the pack of six at the midpoint and only took the lead, as instructed, in the second half of the race. He was muted in his appreciation for what we'd done and told us that next time it would be better still. No one noticed, apart from him, that the cockiness and boredom had, of course, quietly disappeared.'

'Ferguson was like a psychiatrist,' says Neville. 'He had an amazing ability to impact people's minds and handle people differently. You would walk out of his office having been dropped, with a smile on your face. It was extraordinary. Ferguson's ability to handle different people was immense, and it set him apart.'

The great coaches work on you physically and mentally. A good coach will know when to raise the emotional temperature and when to cool things down. They will know when an intervention is required and when less is more. Denise Lewis won gold in the heptathlon at the Sydney Olympics in 2000, and she is clear about the impact her coach Charles van Commenee had on her all-round performance. 'He was hugely performance-motivated,' she says. 'We were both aligned on the goal: winning gold. He always used more carrot than stick with me. He got me to do things I didn't always like; he took me to places I wouldn't have gone to by myself. He was great at getting the best out of me. He lifted the quality of my training and my mental approach ... He knew that I was a good competitor, and so he could be very blunt. He would often use shock value to get me to train as hard as I needed to.'

Coaches, like players, tend to learn the hard way. Tamsin Greenway, one of the UK's leading netball coaches, speaks with great candour about her coaching journey: 'It was 2012 and my first season as player-coach for Surrey Storm. I'd taken on the role with no experience, and it was the first time I'd felt the pressure of leading a team and being alone. As players, you're all in it together; as a coach, it can be lonely and I think you feel as though you fall the hardest. We had a great team and we made the final against Manchester Thunder. I remember at half-time we were level, it was a frustrating game. I came into the changing room in the break and lost it. I don't think I said anything productive; it was more along the lines of, "Be better!" It makes me cringe now, but I was so caught up in the game and the end result I couldn't separate the two. We lost by two goals and I was devastated. I remember standing alone in the changing room after everyone had left and just bursting into tears. I felt a complete failure and that I'd let everyone down. It actually became the making of me as a coach, however. I realised then the importance of player management and of controlling my emotions. I learned that regardless of how I felt at any point as a coach, I couldn't ever project that on to the players.'

There is a balance to be struck here, because showing some emotion or vulnerability in the workplace is not a bad thing per se. A leader who never lowers their guard will often make their direct reports feel inadequate if they betray any signs of stress or anxiety. But what really matters is to be purposeful about how and when you show your emotions. To share that you are frustrated, upset or anxious is completely legitimate if it is authentic, purposeful and done with a projected outcome or response in mind. Sometimes you need to prompt a reaction from your team. Human beings want to work for other human beings, with all their imperfections and vulnerabilities. We build connection with people when we open up and reveal something of ourselves, and showing some emotion can be an effective way of doing that.

CREATE FREEDOM WITH RESPONSIBILITY

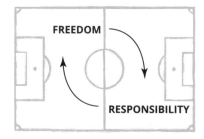

B rian Ashton was the attack coach for Sir Clive Woodward's England team, and he went on to be head coach for the national team. 'Freedom with responsibility' was one of his key mantras, a central pillar of his coaching philosophy. When I spoke with him, he said, 'Coaches require the courage to allow the players freedom to make decisions in the game. Coaches must arm players with intent and then step aside – developing game intelligence is far more important than slavishly following a game plan. It allows players to lead change in real game time.'

The framework demands flexibility of thought and action and the freedom for players to make 'in-game decisions', but it comes with the caveat that players must demonstrate responsibility. In this scenario, coaches become 'enablers' and players act as 'executors'.

A boss who is too controlling will not only stifle the development of their team, they will also stifle the growth of the business. If the leader spends their life signing off every decision and 'marking homework', the organisation will become slow and bureaucratic. In sport, the coach knows that come kick-off time, the team will have to execute, and their ability to influence performance will diminish. In business, there is no such baton pass, and as a consequence, leaders can attempt to control outcomes that are well below their pay grade. The enlightened business leader should be setting the framework, creating the environment and then letting their people crack on. Dana Strong of Comcast built on this point. She said, 'as a leader, your role is to create an environment where problems are solved; it's rarely to solve the problem yourself.'

The British rower Ben Hunt-Davis, who won gold in the men's eight at the Sydney Olympics, was able to operate as an executor thanks to the enabling of his coach. 'In the eight, we did our best to break away from the rest of the [GB rowing] system, so that we could be more ruthless and focused in our learning and decision-making. We simply weren't as good as the guys in the four and pairs, so we had to find a different way of going fast. The person who really drove the change was our crew coach, Martin McElroy. He got great people in around him and he pulled the whole thing together. His style was of getting us to make decisions and take responsibility for what we did and what we chose not to do.'

I think there's a helpful distinction to be made between principles and practices. An organisation that articulates its key principles and beliefs clearly will allow its employees to develop practices that are bespoke and of-the-moment. Being fixed in principle and flexible in practice is a fluid and progressive way to run your business. At the heart of agile teamworking is the ability to create bespoke teams, working to bespoke processes in a dynamic and empowered fashion, and this can only happen if your core principles are locked.

Operational processes that are too rigid will slow you down and create inefficiency. If the playbook is too tightly defined, situational awareness and empowerment will be diminished.

As a team matures, a good coach will evolve their relationship with the team. They will never abdicate authority or responsibility, but they will be able to delegate greater levels of control to the players. Tracey Neville coached the England national netball team to gold in the Commonwealth Games in 2018. She says, 'A key step was giving players the responsibility to change things and adapt on the court. The leadership group learned to control that and manage it well, so that during games, the team became player- rather than coach-led.'

SPECIAL COACHES KNOW HOW TO HANDLE SPECIAL TALENT

Anyone who has watched the Netflix series *The Last Dance* will have observed the diversity of personalities and playing styles that coach Phil Jackson so elegantly managed within an NBA franchise packed with superstars. He would combine Zen Buddhism with Native American history in a relentless balancing of difference and togetherness. He knew when the individual needed to be allowed to express themselves, but he also knew how and when to assert the primacy of the team. He curated a culture, work ethic and code of conduct in the Chicago Bulls that celebrated difference and forged togetherness. For many people, Michael Jordan is the star of the series, but for me it's Phil Jackson. It's a coaching masterclass.

Special coaches know how to handle special talent. They understand that alongside genius, there is often an independence of spirit, insecurity and ego. A good coach will never let their star talent break teamship rules, but they will give them the space and respect that they need to be their best selves. If you try too hard to make a prodigy or a maverick conform, you will put limitations on their ability to perform. They need a clear framework, but they also need the freedom to express themselves. In order to create that kind of freedom, everyone has to be crystal clear on the team's core principles. The coach's message and standards have to be universally understood.

Sir Alex Ferguson was a master at managing this dynamic and allowing special talent to flourish within a culture and framework that he set. Anyone who has read anything about his leadership style will know that he was more multi-dimensional than the media often suggested: it's been said that he could be a visionary, a father figure, a puppet master, and a judge and jury, all in one day. The famous 'hair dryer' treatment was always there, of course, but so was a nurturing and supportive style. The way he supported Eric Cantona after his infamous kung-fu kick on a fan in 1995 is a clear example of this. Ferguson acknowledged that Cantona was special and that he needed special treatment.

It seems that Ferguson would indulge difference, while at the same time having zero tolerance for anyone who crossed the line when it came to his teamship principles. He famously removed his talismanic captain Roy Keane from the club after a TV interview that Ferguson deemed disrespectful.

Ferguson contrasted his varying treatment of players with a

relentlessly consistent team narrative. 'The success and the ability to stay successful was all born out of the manager first and the support of the senior players in the dressing room second,' says Gary Neville. 'There was no escape from the relentless pursuit of winning and giving your all. Ferguson's team talks were all littered with examples about standards and work ethic, repeating that work ethic every single day. He never stopped. And the players became disciples and led it from within.'

Sir Clive Woodward didn't have the same length of tenure that Ferguson did – seven years with England compared to Fergie's 26 years at United – nor the relentless success of Phil Jackson, who won 11 NBA titles. But he did share their core belief that different players needed to be looked after differently.

Lawrence Dallaglio was Clive's first captain, and Clive never forgot that. He knew that Dallaglio had to lose the captaincy after he was embroiled in a scandal, but he also knew that he had a special leader who needed to feel respected and listened to. After Dallaglio resigned the captaincy and stood down from the summer tour in 1999, Martin Johnson took over the captaincy, but Lawrence never stopped leading. Woodward and Dallaglio shared a very special relationship – in many ways, they were closer than Clive and Johnno were.

Jason Robinson switched codes from rugby league to union in November 2000, joining Sale Sharks. Clive knew that he needed Jason's X factor, and Jason won his first cap three months later. Jason's family and his faith both played a major role in his life, and Clive allowed his family to stay with him at Pennyhill Park in advance of matches. No other team members had family staying with them during competitions, but it mattered to Jason, so it mattered to Clive.

Jason recalls this incredible piece of man management very fondly: 'The ability to have my family with me – and I knew it was a special request that was afforded to no one else – meant everything to me, and Clive knew how important it was to me. By supporting me, he got my complete loyalty – that was me in my happy place. In order for me to do what I did, that's what I needed to happen. You need that understanding. We're not all robots – we need that flexibility, no matter how strong we think we are. He backed me and I gave him 100 per cent.'

Though Jonny Wilkinson had none of the behaviours of a superstar, he was as important to our team as Tom Brady was to the New England Patriots or Virat Kohli is to the Indian cricket team. Clive was extraordinarily protective of his young prodigy, showing him a real sense of reverence and care. Woodward could be tough and short with some players, but never with Wilko. He knew that nobody was tougher on themselves than Jonny was, and in fact he sometimes needed to protect Jonny from himself.

Clive knew that he needed to give Wilko support and confidence. Jonny was given a one-to-one minder in Dave Alred, who became his kicking coach, mentor, technical adviser and training buddy. Jonny was also granted special access to practise his kicking at Twickenham, as if it were his own personal playground. If a left-field suggestion was introduced to the group, there was a sense that Clive would glance over to Jonny and see if there was a smile or a look of dread. Wilko was even given a special golden bib to wear on occasion, which meant nobody could touch him. I used to look at it in the hope that one Tuesday, our contact day, it would be offered to me. I'm still waiting . . .

If we were to draw out one characteristic shared by these legendary coaches, it is their ability to balance a singular mission and narrative with a diverse approach to the personalities in their team – to set a purpose and develop a winning style while embracing special and prodigious talent. They are coaches of the body and the mind – multi-dimensional leaders who know how to embrace difference and forge togetherness.

World-Class Coaching: Highlights

1. Have both your telescope and microscope to hand. The best leaders can switch from small detail to big picture in a heartbeat.

2. Manage by mantra: keep things simple and memorable.

3. Keep it positive! Focus your language on the upside, and the results might surprise you.

4. Warm things up and cool them down when necessary. Gauging and managing the emotional and psychological temperature of your people reaps dividends.

5. Coaches are enablers and players are executors. A confident relationship between player and coach pays tenfold.

6. Indulge your mavericks, but understand when it's necessary to put the team first.

7. Create freedom within a framework. Get clear on your strategic intent and fixed principles so you can unleash your talent.

8. Culture

*'Culture is what people do when
no one is looking.'*

DIFFERENCE   TOGETHERNESS   GROWTH

At international level, rugby teams embrace their collective and cultural difference. When playing at their best, they celebrate a distinctive national style; a style that is handed down over generations and is often an embodiment of their culture and history. It pays to respect and embrace these traits.

This style can be evolved, of course, but you can't get an Aussie team to play like a Springbok team, or encourage the French to fight against the gravitational pull of their national style of play. It is when the French are the most 'French' that they are the most lethal – there's a whole generation of All Blacks who will tell you that.

Let's take a whistle-stop tour around the rugby world, looking at the four teams who have won World Cups and another one that should have.

When I think of Australia, I immediately recall the classic *Blackadder* sketch in which Rowan Atkinson's title character asks about a cunning plan: 'As cunning as a fox who's just been appointed professor of cunning at Oxford University?' There is no better way to describe the Aussies on a rugby field. They can have you chasing shadows as they seem to perform magic tricks with the ball, making it disappear up one sleeve and come out from behind your ear. As a young student of the game, I marvelled at the Ella brothers, David Campese and Michael Lynagh, then Tim Horan and later George Gregan, Stephen Larkham and

Joe Roff; teams like the Queensland Reds in the 1990s and the Brumbies at the start of the new millennium. I would devour tapes to see big men facing them utterly bamboozled by their creativity. What was so compelling was that it was all done with the nonchalance of a beach bum throwing a ball around on Manly Beach. The Wallabies ask you more questions than any other team – playing against them is mentally exhausting.

Playing against the South Africans is physically exhausting. They are massive and they respect no one, especially a team who won't stand up to them physically. They will find your weakness and they will intimidate you. They will keep getting up off the floor and coming again. They will shut down your space and try to starve the game of oxygen. At its best, Springbok rugby is built on a huge forward pack with a metronomic set piece. There will be a fly half who can kick further than Rory McIlroy can hit a golf ball. They love a drop goal. They will pin you deep, they will hurt you and then they will repeat the process. It isn't always pretty, but it is brutally effective.

When the French click, they can beat anyone. The south-west of France produces specimens who can go toe-to-toe with any world pack, and they've always produced backs who can get the crowd to its feet. The French game has been built on an aware-ness of space and a willingness to play from anywhere and to counter-attack. They have a selflessness in their backlines that allows the ball to be the true champion when they attack. To watch them offload and support is like watching ballet. Their juxtaposition of brutality and art makes for an intoxicating Gal-lic cocktail.

And what about the proud English? Well, the English at their best are a side built to deny opponents the ball. To control and dominate set pieces. To kick, turn a team and then press. No question, they have had regal 'flyers' behind the scrum: Jeremy

Guscott, Jason Robinson and Jonny May are as good as anything the game has seen. But the classic description of an English rugby team would start with Dean Richards, Martin Johnson, Maro Itoje, Billy Vunipola, Jonny Wilkinson, Rob Andrew and Owen Farrell. These are unbreakable men of few words and giant deeds, the kind of men Wellington would have lined up behind. Masters of close combat who bring order to chaos, our heroes wear the number one to ten jerseys. The Heavy Brigade grind the opposition down and then, when the chance comes, they release the flyers.

Even though the Springboks have won as many World Cups, it is fair to say that over the past 30 years, New Zealand have consistently been the best side in the world. When they are at their best, they can match the physicality of the Springboks, the skill levels of the Wallabies and the cussed defiance of the English – they are a perfect hybrid of the leading rugby nations. Hugely aggressive but also clinical, passionate and precise. The All Blacks jersey has a huge multiplier effect on performance – no one wants to let it down. They do the simple things better than anyone in the world. They have beautiful, natural ball-handling, and they move the ball around the contact area with devastating pace. They do the ordinary things extraordinarily well, and at such great speed that they can be impossible to defend against for a full 80 minutes. It is their ability to beat you physically and mentally that makes them the most successful sporting team in the world; they have the highest win ratio of any country, in any sport. They have created a culture of excellence that endures beyond any individual.

A great company will nurture and protect its culture. It will understand that this mysterious and intangible asset, although hard to quantify, powers colleague pride and performance. Human beings like to feel that we are part of a community that shares our values and beliefs, and this sense of belonging is often fuelled more by the culture of an organisation than by the products and services it creates. The challenger spirit of Virgin; the innovation of Apple; the engineering heritage of Audi: these are ideas and mindsets that galvanise people together, the pillars upon which the culture is built and sustained. They are built slowly, with actions and deeds. Although a culture is always evolving and shifting, a smart organisation will use its past to help navigate its future. The old-timers will invest time in new joiners, telling them the stories that matter. Just as it is with purpose, when it comes to building and sustaining culture, this connection between old and new is critical. You want to forge a connection between the wisest veterans and the freshest recruits.

USE YOUR PAST TO HELP NAVIGATE YOUR FUTURE

The Wallabies have created a great tradition around World Cup selection. A player who has made the squad will receive a phone call from a Wallaby great informing them that they have been selected. So George Gregan might ring Will Genia, or John

Eales might call a young second row. Unlike the first cap ceremony at the start of the first day in Test match cricket, these conversations are private, and I'm told they can last for some time. It's a wonderful way of connecting the Wallabies' past and present and investing in the culture.

A strong culture draws the best from its past, using its own history to navigate its future. Like the words in a stick of rock, the core values run through a strong culture. Why is the SAS training headquarters at Hereford named after its founder, David Stirling? It's called Stirling Lines so that the deeds and beliefs of the regiment's founding members are never forgotten – so that those warriors in the North African deserts are connected to the special forces of today. These elite cultures understand that some things can change, while some absolutely mustn't. Think of the commitment to design at Apple or to creativity at Pixar. Remove those things and you've removed the keystone of the whole organisation.

When a proud business loses its way it's often because it has drifted away from its cultural keystone. The start of the recovery can often be the reconnection of the business with its historical DNA.

Dave Lewis describes how this happened at Tesco: 'Customer-centricity is at the heart of the culture at Tesco. We just went back to doing the right thing for customers. At Tesco, leadership reminded the business that it was customer-centricity that had driven its growth in the past, and that customer-centricity would be the key to its future.'

The England rugby team creates an environment in which there are constant inspiring reminders of the culture ingrained within the team's DNA. In the tunnel at Twickenham, the phrase 'Remember who stood here' was written in big, bold letters. We had plaques on the wall listing England's greatest victories. As a player you wanted to add to that wall, to leave your own mark and make your own history. The changing room there now fuses the past with the present. There are hi-tech cryotherapy chambers alongside the old baths. At each player's locker are the names of the ten greatest players to have played in that position. As you leave the dressing room, a grey wall is engraved with all the greatest victories, scorelines and players, complete with their number of caps and tries. Opposite, in the tunnel, there are pictures of the current crop with the words that mean everything to them. An acknowledgement of the past, but a focus on the present.

Every six months, BBH ran an induction process called Dunk. In that session, the 40 or so most recent joiners would listen to a presentation from Sir Nigel Bogle about the history of the company and its values and beliefs. The presentation would finish with drinks and a dinner, where the newbies were joined by an equal number of carefully chosen longer-serving employees. Ben says that he always liked the idea of taking the budget that might have been used for 'leaving drinks' and spending it on 'joining drinks'. The idea was that you were metaphorically 'dunking' the new joiners into the culture, accelerating their sense of understanding and belonging. You were teaching them about BBH's history so they were better able to navigate its future.

STRONG CULTURES ARE BUILT
ON AND OFF THE PITCH

The bonds between team members are built by shared endeavour on the pitch, but also by downtime spent away from it. When I was an England player, we had a cinema trip every Friday. Wherever we were in the world, a group of us that invariably included Ben Cohen, Steve Thompson, Lewis Moody and I would go to the cinema and make the inevitable trip to the foyer for popcorn, Tango and a bag of Minstrels for Jason Leonard. A trip to the zoo was more up the street of Jonny Wilkinson and Richard Hill – there can't be many in the world they haven't seen.

Just as important a ritual was 'Wednesday night calamari'. As sports science and nutrition began to take over and the approach became more professional, the fridges of our hotel bedrooms were emptied of chocolate and alcohol; side orders of chips with dinner disappeared as an option; and the hot chocolate with scones and cream was culled from the physio room.

When we stayed at Pennyhill Park, the England rugby training base in Surrey, we would escape the bubble and head to Casa Nova, an Italian restaurant in Virginia Water. As the senior player, Jason Leonard would be left to sign off what was often an eye-watering bill at the end of the meal. There would be calamari, buffalo mozzarella, platefuls of spaghetti carbonara, pizza after pizza and Mark Regan's umpteen portions of *gambas*. And then came the puddings – chocolate in all forms, cake or ice cream. It was everything you shouldn't eat. Heavy carbohydrates after 8pm, sugary puddings, alcohol – all in moderation, I hasten to add. But we left the sports science and the rugby at the door, no matter who our opponents were on the Saturday. If we were away from home, our sensational team manager Louise Ramsay and the senior players would source a restaurant to fit our brief: large portions, a nice area to ourselves and speedy service.

It was on these evenings that the bonds of teamship were made, when the talk moved away from defence and lineout calls to everything from family to football. You hung out with the people – not the players – and found out what made them tick. In team sports, the time away from the big stadiums and training pitches, getting to know your colleagues and teammates, goes a long way to determining how you perform.

The better you understand the person, the better you will understand the player or the executive. Sometimes, an apparently small fact from someone's back story will unlock your understanding of them, so why not find out about their upbringing and education, their hopes and fears, their sense of humour? These conversations and the subsequent learnings are not indulgences; they are the mortar that binds the bricks of teamship together.

Ben's first four years as CEO of BBH in Asia took him all over the region, as he met clients in Bangkok, Shanghai, Jakarta and Tokyo. One of the things he learned was the power of the client dinner, and the amount of work that could often be done outside of the meeting room. Because your clients know that you've flown in, a dinner would often be offered after the meeting. Ben would try to flip this and get the dinner to happen the night before the meeting. A much more convivial and relaxed environment would then transpire, in which he could cover all the important agenda items, making the formal meeting a 'rubber-stamping' exercise. It had the additional advantage of giving the most senior decision-maker a 'private view' before they were asked to make a decision in front of their team. Wining and dining clients is increasingly seen as 'old-school', but over the course of a two-hour dinner, you do the business, but you also do a great deal more. You talk family, holidays, sport and politics. You create context and you build connection.

I spoke to the international cricketer and 2019 World Cup winner Jos Buttler about long tours spent away from loved ones. He said, 'One of the best things I found on the ODI tour to the West Indies was that if ever someone put a message on the team WhatsApp group that they were going out for a drink or a meal, nearly everyone who didn't have a commitment would be there. Out of a squad of 15, there were nearly always 12 lads joining up in the evenings, very organically and off the cuff, to enjoy each other's company. It may seem a small moment in the grand scheme of things, but it struck me that I'd never been in a team before where that mateship was so genuine and people just wanted to spend time together. It brought us all even tighter as a group, our enjoyment levels were high, and it reflected in our performances on the field.'

One of the business challenges of remote working is that work can become very transactional. During the periods of lockdown during the Covid-19 pandemic, many people observed that they had plenty of human contact, but they missed the human connection of face to face working. People began to crave the five-minute chat before a meeting or the informal lunch. The efficiency of Zoom meetings and Google Hangouts can begin to take a toll on your connections, and consequently your culture.

At BBH, Ben always took the big annual set pieces very seriously. Christmas company meetings and parties were planned as if they were the Oscars. One year, the Christmas party had a *Strictly Come Dancing* theme, and six BBH-ers spent three months secretly training with professional dancers so that they could impress their colleagues on the big night. The whole evening was true to the TV format, with behind-the-scenes video footage, interviews and a panel of BBH-ers and celebrity judges. This might sound expensive and over the top, but such events created cultural capital and social currency.

We said earlier that the contribution of culture is hard to quantify, but there are three areas we would point to: recruitment, retention and performance. Firstly, recruitment. The employer's brand really matters, and stories about your culture can impact it faster and more effectively than anything else. The big set pieces are expensive in time and money, but they help with recruitment and strengthen your reputation as an employer. The quality of the food on Google's Mountain View campus, which became famous in Silicon Valley, is a great example of this. You might think of this as a small or environmental factor, but it became a point of competitive difference. The founders Larry Page and Sergey Brin clearly knew what Napoleon knew: an army marches on its stomach.

Secondly, when it comes to the retention of top talent, the bottom line is impacted in two ways: you spend less time and money on recruitment, and the talent that you've trained builds their career with you rather than somewhere else. Of course you want some churn, but losing talent that you've nurtured is both painful and expensive.

Finally, performance. Ben's leadership group believed passionately that staff engagement and pride were strategically critical to the success of the business, because enthusiastic employees were more courageous, curious and creative. BBH chairman Jim Carroll coined the phrase 'Positive people have bigger, better ideas.'

Looked at through this lens, these big events become investments rather than costs. With an event like 'BBH Does *Strictly*', you are making big deposits of positive capital in the culture, which can be drawn upon during tough times that may lie ahead.

I CAN'T HEAR YOUR WORDS BECAUSE YOUR ACTIONS ARE DEAFENING ME

As young footballers, the Manchester United Class of '92 – David Beckham, Nicky Butt, Gary and Phil Neville, Ryan Giggs and Paul Scholes – were inducted into a first-team squad that featured a good deal of bullying as part of its culture. Scholes was famously locked in a kit bag during an away trip. I'm sure it was all dressed up as 'banter' and part of the young lads' 'apprenticeship', but as the Class of '92 matured, they decided to do away with it. Gary Neville described their reasons: 'When we became more senior, we believed in the togetherness and spirit garnered from soft initiations, but it had gone too far and we believed that for a group to grow with the right spirit, it needed to be done within reason and for a better purpose.'

From a position of power and influence, the Class of '92 changed a negative aspect of the culture. It reminds me of something I was once told by a wise schoolmaster: 'Your children won't do what you say, but they will do what you do.' It is the behaviours and habits that you might not even be aware of that influence the culture.

In the workplace, good habits are aped, just as bad ones are. If the most senior person tidies the meeting room or makes a cup of tea for their PA, others will follow. Likewise, if the most senior leaders communicate that it's acceptable to bang the table and shout and scream, then that's what you're going to see more of.

'Cultures are always talked about, but they are seldom lived,' says Dave Lewis. 'A saying at Tesco is "People watch your feet, not your lips." Your actions matter more than your words. I quote Stephen Covey often: "You can't talk your way out of a problem you've behaved your way into." '

Aligning around a code of conduct in a business team will help you to define your behaviours. Companies spend an awful lot of time defining their 'why' (the purpose) and their 'what' (the mission), but not enough on their 'how'.

One of the exercises that Ben facilitates with a leadership team is defining the behaviours that they want to role-model. You might describe this as a code of conduct or a teamship charter. In this process, colleagues make commitments to each other regarding 'how' the team is going to carry itself and determine which behaviours will be acceptable and which will not. The commitment to a code of conduct is a statement that values and behaviours matter, and that it's not OK to get the job done at any cost. It is my belief that bullying and selfish behaviours may work in the short term, but they will be found out in the long term.

It's hard to create this kind of asset in the abstract, and Ben's company The Growth House has found that it's much more productive to start with individuals' beliefs and then to aggregate them. When building a teamship charter, Ben starts by asking questions. What are the behaviours that will get the very best out of you? What will get the very worst? What are the behaviours you want to foster in the teams that you lead? As the charter starts to emerge, it's important to keep your language simple and free of cliché. It's also important to discuss what your 'red lines' are, to agree the consequences of breaking this charter and how the team will hold each other to account.

Jeff Dodds of Virgin Media says: 'Lots of people join us because they have a strong idea of what a Virgin business is. We champion the customer. We do things differently. We have fun. As a consequence, our culture is not really set from the top. The job of the people at the top then becomes to deliver on the culture that our people expect and demand from a Virgin business. In leadership, you can't tell people what you are and then behave in a way that is different to that. It's very jarring in any culture if your behaviours don't match your narrative, but it's particularly so in ours. My dad had a phrase that I use often: "I can't hear your words because your actions are deafening me."'

Whether the culture is powered top-down or bottom-up, leaders need to be aware of the impact of their behaviours. 'Culture is created by everyone,' says the ITV CEO Carolyn McCall, 'but leaders have to remember that they are always being looked at. If you're trying to foster a collaborative culture but not living that as a senior team, it won't stick – it just won't be credible. You have to work all the time at the signals you are sending, even with your body language.'

Former Ireland captain Paul O'Connell takes this idea even further. He describes a good culture as being one where 'the team coaches itself by creating good habits'. He describes how the players in the Munster squad would arrive at training 30 minutes before the session started to work on their own specialist skills, with no coaches in sight. Over time, new players would pick up this habit because that was what everyone else was doing. Human beings will mirror each other, for better or worse.

CULTURE CAN BE HARD TO CHANGE, BUT IT CAN ALSO BE FRAGILE

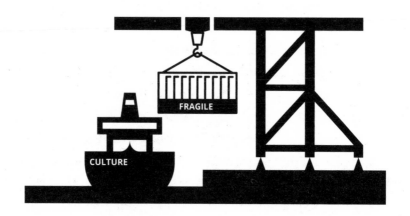

The business guru Peter Drucker famously said, 'Culture eats strategy for breakfast.' The point he was making is that the invisible forces that exist within a company, built over many years, are often hard to change. A culture almost always has good and bad characteristics. It might be fiercely intelligent but bordering on the intellectual, or high in performance but low on praise and acknowledgement. It might be rigorous and robust but a little slow. The leadership team should try to amplify the strengths and work on the weaknesses.

Despite being hard to change, culture can also be fragile. It can be undermined by small details, damaged in little increments as standards slip and negative behaviours creep in. The All Blacks famously have a 'no dickheads' policy in their team – they know that a few rotten apples can spoil the whole barrel. They know that strong cultures are built slowly but damaged quickly.

A capable coach or leader must act quickly and decisively if they feel that the group's values or culture are under threat. Jack

Welch, the legendary CEO of General Electric, famously talked about four kinds of executives:

- Those who get the values and do the numbers.
- Those who don't get the values and don't do the numbers.
- Those who get the values but don't do the numbers.
- Those who do the numbers but don't get the values.

The sky's the limit for the first group, while the second obviously go and the third get a second chance. Welch claimed that the fourth group – people who 'kiss up and kick down' – are the most dangerous in any company. They have to go because 'they have the power to destroy the open, informal, trust-based culture that we need to win today and tomorrow'. Well said, Jack.

Rich Pierson of Headspace echoes the sentiment. 'They say that culture is what people do when you're not looking,' he says, 'so you need to be very clear about what you are and what you aren't. The work we've done on the values has really helped. We looked at the people who we felt displayed our culture best and we explored their characteristics. We then articulated three two-word couplets: "Selfless drive." "Courageous heart." "Curious mind."

'It's the combination of the words that makes them powerful. Launched about four years ago, they now drive how we reward, appraise and hire. We have a bonus system that allows peers to bonus each other according to these values.'

Many of the words used by big businesses to describe themselves all tend to be the same. What's great about the phrases that Headspace has created is that they each contain some tension. To be selfless *and* to have drive; to be courageous *and* kind-hearted. I see it as the balance and harmony of Buddhism expressing itself.

Bad habits become ingrained in a culture just as good habits do, and there has to be a clear line to determine what will be tolerated. Ben recalls that his toughest conversations as CEO were never to do with performance interventions, but rather when a cultural or behavioural 'red line' had been crossed. The golden rule of feedback is 'Be tough on the issue and soft on the person', but when it comes to behaviours that damage the culture, he argues that it's perfectly acceptable to be tough on both.

STORIES ARE THE ORIGINAL SOCIAL MEDIA

For thousands of years, human beings have told stories. Stories are how we teach, how we learn and how we explain the values and culture of our tribe. In a strong culture, stories are passed on from generation to generation.

Paul O'Connell explains that Sir Ian McGeechan, the legendary British and Irish Lions player and coach, is a great storyteller. 'He has a story for every occasion, and he uses them to explain the history and culture of the Lions. At the start of the tour to South Africa in 2009, he chose to tell us all about how incredible Jason Leonard was after being dropped to the bench in 1997 while Paul Wallace started ahead of him at tighthead. He calls him "the ultimate Lion". You sit there thinking, "If I don't make the Test team, I want to play that Jason Leonard role."'

If I was to pick a single story that defined the defiance of the England team I played in, it would be Dublin in 2003, when we lined up on the left of the red carpet to meet the dignitaries before the anthems, upsetting the Irish because that was 'their side'. We were asked to move, but that was never going to happen – Martin Johnson decided that we would not take a backward step even before the kick-off. Neil Back walked up and down our line like Bill Sikes's dog. 'No one moves,' he said, as Johnno continued his 'discussions' with the officials. It wasn't the Irish team, fans or media I was worried about – it was what Neil Back would do to me if I moved. When Martin Johnson told you to get off the floor and make the next tackle, you did it. That's a team. That's a culture.

Great leaders are often great storytellers. They know that stories do a number of things all at once. They make teaching practical and real, taking theory and turning it into practice. They also make things personal; they allow the leader to share part of themselves, to show vulnerability, emotion and humour. Stories are made for sharing – the teller gives their own unique perspective on what they have heard – and they build connection and community.

A culture is created by its stories. If their protagonists demonstrate great creativity, salesmanship or resilience, these are the values that you are elevating. And the same is true if they tell of humility and kindness. A leader who proudly speaks of working through holidays and weekends and being the first in the office and the last out, is communicating very clearly what kind of culture they want to build.

At a time when companies are looking to reduce their costs, they should be mindful that a strong culture amplifies and increases value. It reduces churn and the cost of staff replacement, it increases colleague pride and productivity, and it builds reputational strength and advocacy.

As the nature of work evolves and we embrace remote working, the creation and maintenance of culture will be a key leadership challenge. Many of the tactics and tools for building it have relied on face-to-face engagement and physical proximity – our office spaces have often played a key role in this, as has time spent nearby for a start-of-week coffee or an end-of-week drink. In a world of Webex and Zoom, this kind of connection is harder to create.

Sir Nigel Bogle believes that in the future, people will do 'more work at home and more play at work'. I think the point he's making is deeply profound. He's suggesting that offices will become less about workstations and daily endeavour, and more about connectivity and culture. Our face-to-face time might take place weekly rather than daily, with work spaces being for 'checking in' and collaborative problem-solving. If the role of offices diminishes, it will be even more important that we invest in culture, shared identity and belonging. What a leadership challenge. What an opportunity.

World-Class Culture: Highlights

1. When it comes to culture, actions speak louder than words.

2. Create a code of conduct to establish which behaviours are acceptable and which are not.

3. Strong cultures are built on *and* off the pitch: know the person, and you will know the player.

4. Use your past to help navigate your future, and dunk new people into the culture to get them swimming in the same direction as quickly as possible.

5. Your culture can be a point of difference from your competitors, powering recruitment, retention and performance.

6. The culture creates the sense of tribe. If different types of people don't feel a sense of belonging, it's time to look at your culture.

7. Stories make teaching practical and real; they create connection and community. A culture is sustained through the stories it tells.

9. Communication

*'My eyes were a weapon, but without
my mouth they were blunt. Good teams
over-communicate.'*

DIFFERENCE | TOGETHERNESS | GROWTH

Now that I've retired, people often ask me what I miss most about the game. Scoring a try? The feeling of winning a tough contest? Performing in front of a huge crowd in the biggest stadiums? These are all valid suggestions, but none of them are correct. What I miss most is the buzz of the changing room ten minutes before kick-off.

First there was the silence, broken by the rattle of studs on the floor as players retreated into themselves for their final individual reflections. Then the orators went to work. Lawrence Dallaglio was like the East End hardman Lenny McLean, all grimace and jutting jaw. Matt Dawson would be there with the tactics, while Neil Back yapped away in bursts. The giant silverback Jason Leonard offered a simple hug to let you know that he was with you.

Martin Johnson would be on the edge of it all, avoiding the spotlight until it was his time. Then he would walk to the centre of the changing room, knowing that his gravitational pull would make us form a circle around him. He would stand in the middle, slowly rotating so that nobody spent long looking at his giant back, and eyeball every single one of us, his stare letting us know that he would do whatever needed to be done. 'You'd better be with me,' his eyes would say, all before he'd even opened his mouth. We would have followed him anywhere.

There were so many different types of communication in those final minutes, and they would combine to create the perfect cocktail of focus and readiness. Leadership is more about action than words, but communication plays a critical role. And when your actions and narrative are completely aligned, you will be very hard to beat.

The place to start when you're thinking about communication, with both large and small groups, is how you want to make people feel. If you start with your desired outcomes, the task of defining your inputs becomes a good deal easier. Human beings feel just as much as we think, so your communication needs to be a blend of the rational and the emotional. It's always a cocktail of what we say, how it's being said and who is saying it.

Do you want people to feel energised and inspired? Do you want to show that you empathise and that you've really listened? Or do you want people to feel challenged and to take greater accountability for their performance?

I've spent nearly 20 years as a broadcaster following my retirement, so I've thought a great deal about how to connect with large audiences while still trying to keep things personal. A great broadcaster makes you feel as if they are communicating directly with you. They make their words feel intimate, as if they are sitting in your living room. Good punditry talks to a broad church, respecting the knowledgeable fan but also connecting with the newest recruit, and this core objective is the same when speaking to a business audience. You need to give insight and expertise, while also making it feel accessible. You need your messages to connect at a personal level. It's an obvious point to make, but a large audience is no more than a collection of individuals.

What's exciting to me is that we never stop developing our communication skills. Ideally, we pick up things that we like from others, finding tools and techniques that work for us, but most importantly we find our own voice. There's no right or wrong way when it comes to communication – only what's right for you.

Of all the chapters in this book, this one could be a book in itself. But we are going to try to practise what we preach and look at the five most important principles of communicating with impact.

HIGH-PERFORMANCE TEAMS OVER-COMMUNICATE

Good teams are noisy. They share what they are seeing, using communication to intimidate the opposition with their constant transfer of information.

I took my local club team Maidenhead RFC to train against the Barbarians. It was a blistering session, and when I asked the lads for feedback afterwards, they all talked about the same two things: the communication and the speed. 'Why was there so much noise?' they asked.

'Because all that noise is information,' I said, 'and good information makes you faster. It allows the players around you to gain a broader perspective, faster. It arms decision-makers with the full topography of the battlefield.' The communication and the speed were inextricably linked. They powered each other.

When I'm asked how I learned to commentate on television, I always respond by saying that it was simply a continuation of how I played. I was always talking: passing on information and processing it internally by thinking out loud. My eyes were a weapon, but without my mouth they were blunt. I suspect that Jonny Wilkinson wanted to tell me to shut up on many occasions, but I knew that the more I told him about the shapes and scenarios I could see, the faster and better his decision-making would be.

Good teams also over-communicate in the workplace. They are constantly checking in, sharing small wins and minor setbacks. High levels of communication give team members different perspectives on any given issue, as well as creating shared understanding and connectedness. The downside is also true: the fastest way to create silos and division within a business is to stop communicating.

You can hear the buzz of a good team when you enter their working area. A weekend anecdote might be shared or a boxset recommended; it's the sound of human connection. Communication between the team shouldn't filter exclusively through the leader; there should be a spider's web of connectedness, although it is the leader's job to set the tone. If they are secretive and reluctant to share information, this behaviour will be mirrored; if they are open and high-contact, the same will also be true.

In a review or 'wash up' of something that has gone wrong in the workplace, the root cause is often poor communication: 'That wasn't clear', 'I hadn't heard that' or 'I heard that differently'. A team with a growth mindset will understand that communication can be developed and trained like any other skill.

A good leader will think about which messages they want to be 'broadcast' and which ones require a 'narrowcast' approach – the things they will share as a group and those that require a private dialogue. Our response to a piece of news is often conditioned by the timing, the environment and the manner in which it is received. 'It wasn't so much what I heard, but how I heard it.' 'It just would have been nice to have been told in advance.' 'I always seem to be the last person to find out.' These classic grievances are all completely avoidable.

For the big set pieces and important moments, I've found it helpful to ask three simple questions about the communication plan:

- What exactly is our message?
- How exactly are we telling people?
- Who exactly is doing which conversation?

It is always worth spending time answering these questions because it's easy to mess up a good message with poor delivery. This is why a good comms or PR person is so invaluable at the top of an organisation. They will interrogate the message in a strategic way, but they will also help you to craft the execution and delivery of that message.

A good leader will often have a person in their team who is expert at preparing the ground for a piece of messaging to land, and then following up afterwards with reassurance and clarification. In the spirit of over-communicating, it's helpful to think about what work you want to be done before and after an announcement.

Sometimes there will be issues around confidentiality and timing that mean communication has to be carefully choreographed. In these situations, it is important to create forums and opportunities to follow up. The most natural and authentic communicators are often the most effective, but there will be times when your messaging needs to be precise, for example around a redundancy process. If you operate in leadership for long enough, you will eventually have to execute one of these – and it will test your communication skills like nothing else.

In such situations, the leader and the team need to craft their narrative carefully and remain consistent and aligned. In these moments, you have to control the dialogue; you have to try to shape the narrative, rather than letting it control you.

TRY TO CONTROL THE DIALOGUE
AND STAY ON-MESSAGE

Warren Gatland, the much-celebrated Kiwi coach who has teams like Wasps, Wales and the British and Irish Lions on his CV, commands fierce loyalty from his players. Crucially, he is a brilliant communicator, and I used to marvel at his performance in press conferences. He would take progressive actions like holding training camps in Poland and using cryotherapy chambers. What became most interesting was not so much what Gatland's teams were doing, but how they would communicate about these activities. They would talk about them as if they gave his team superpowers. He said that his team was the fittest in the world. His players believed it, the media, and it soon became a self-fulfilling prophecy. The opposition couldn't help but hear it, and the Welsh players fed off it. There's a great story about the team strength and conditioning coach Paul Stridgeon telling the Welsh lads that the water they were drinking was special. It was all nonsense, of course, but the players genuinely believed they were getting an edge because of their special water. Warren is a master at controlling the dialogue and always seems able to take the conversation to where he wants it to go.

Before you can share a message, you need to craft it. Writing is the obvious place to start, but that can only get you so far – there comes a point when you can only test your narrative by saying it out loud, in front of an audience. Things that might look great on paper might not land correctly live, while important messages might be in the wrong order or have the wrong emphasis.

I once watched a documentary on the making of the TV sitcom *Friends* and was struck that after an exhaustive writing and rehearsal process, the show was always shot in front of a studio audience. They did this because if a joke wasn't working, it would be rewritten and reshot – the producers would literally test out jokes and then rework and rerecord them. They baked the audience response into the creative development process.

Similarly, in the US presidential election, candidates use the early primaries and caucuses to refine and craft their message. Over time, candidates have learned that they will only really know how their narrative sounds and how it lands when they try it on a live audience. For many years, I never understood why you see big-name politicians addressing groups of 10 or 20 people in their front rooms, until someone explained that they are beta-testing their positions. They are researching language and ideas in real time. They emerge from this first stage of the exhaustive process with their message crafted and tested.

The cast of *Friends* and presidential hopefuls are following the same process. Because no matter what you're trying to communicate – a joke, presidential potential or a business pitch – the principle remains the same. Crafting and refining 'in rehearsal' is priceless when you get to the main event.

With your narrative crafted and tested, the next part of the task is one of consistency and repetition. Alan Jope, the CEO of Unilever, makes this point powerfully:

> When you are leading about a hundred people or less, you can be quite nuanced in your leadership and communication style. When you get over that number, and you are leading hundreds and even thousands of people, your leadership style has to evolve. Your messaging has to become boringly clear and consistent. Just at the point I'm absolutely sick of the sound of my own narrative, it will just be starting to stick. There is causal relationship between the speed of a changing world and the need for consistency of message when you're trying to change big systems.

Some leaders don't just control the dialogue – they create new language. Eddie Jones brilliantly reframed the vocabulary around the subs bench by calling them 'finishers'. This clever use of language completely changes the way the substitutes are viewed by others, and the way they view themselves. They are no longer the spare guys who didn't quite make the starting side; suddenly, they are the black belts who you want to close out the game.

Eddie took this thinking even further at the 2019 World Cup in Japan. History has always dictated that you announce the starting team first and those on the bench second. But before the semi-final against New Zealand, Eddie flipped this on its head. He announced the finishers first, the people that he wanted to close out the game.

For the lads on the bench, the disappointment of not starting was massively diminished by this reframing of their role. Numbers 16 to 23 had been announced first because they were going to be crucial to the outcome of the game. It was a masterstroke.

WORDS ARE ONLY ONE PART OF COMMUNICATION

While writing this book, Ben and I have spent a lot of time and energy crafting the visuals with our designer Emily. We live in a highly visual world, and pictures can often do more than words. Sir John Hegarty, co-founder of BBH, would mischievously call words 'a barrier to communication'. As you may have guessed, he was an art director and not a copywriter.

Lawrence Dallaglio was one of the great communicators. He exuded confidence and self-belief. With Wasps and England, his teammates would follow him anywhere. The jutting jaw, the shoulders, the tears – Dallaglio was a world-class communicator. He could play a bit too, of course. He won everything there is to win in rugby: European cups, domestic titles, a World Cup, Lions series and even a sevens World Cup. When you ask him about the leadership attribute that he thinks is most important, he goes to communication first.

'If the leader's energy and body language isn't at the highest possible level, what hope has your team got?' he says. 'How you carry yourself as the leader really matters. The best way to inspire others is in the energy and positivity that you exude. In the same way that you feed off other people, they feed off you. The greatest gift you can give others is your energy.'

In the workplace, leaders forget that they are being watched by their staff at their peril. Nobody wants to see a concerned-looking pilot flying the plane; they want to see composure and confidence. Leaders need to think carefully about their body language and their energy, not least because it will be mirrored.

And then there's the form of non-verbal communication that is most often overlooked: silence. Great communicators understand how to use silence. They know that standing silently in front of a mic and waiting will quieten a rowdy crowd, and that it can be used to create intensity and drama. In those moments, silence is your friend, so embrace it.

Not everyone loves public speaking. The great Churchillian speech is not possible for most of us, so it's important to find your own voice. You might communicate better in writing than in speaking. You might prefer one-to-ones over big groups, or sitting down to present rather than standing up. Some people like simple headlines in front of them when they communicate their message to the room, while others work best from a script. Over time, you will figure out what works for you and what doesn't. You'll also learn that words are only one item in your toolbox.

The challenge is to find the style and the platforms that suit you best. The only thing that matters is that you do what makes you feel confident and comfortable. I once worked with a CEO who would prepare his team for big presentations by getting them to reduce their PowerPoint decks to a single page of A4. When all the numbers that mattered were on one piece of paper, he would get them to put it away. In that final stage, with the homework done, he just wanted them to get their heads up and tell the story. He wanted accuracy, of course, but he also wanted conviction and confidence.

Great presenters use charts and notes, but they use them to support their storytelling. I am always meticulous about my preparation and rehearsal so that I can get my head up and present in as natural and confident a fashion as possible.

OUR NEW WORLD MAY REQUIRE SOME NEW SKILLS

During the Covid-19 pandemic, many high-performing teams recognised not just the importance of increased communication, but the requirement to evolve their communication skills for a remote working environment. As Webex and Zoom meetings complement and replace face-to-face interaction, a number of things have started to emerge. Some of them are positive, but others are much less so.

Firstly, we've learned that the dynamic of a multi-person video call is fine for lots of the tasks that constitute 'business as usual', but a poor medium for complex problem-solving. It is hard to create the environment of a classic brainstorm when you're working remotely. In these meetings, you want to be able to interrupt each other, to build and to do lots of things that are really hard over a computer. On a video call, the baton tends to be passed from person to person, and the meeting becomes a series of monologues rather than a fluid dialogue. Anything you can do to break up this kind of staccato communication is worth it.

Secondly, people have learned that there is real value in the classic one-to-one phone call. Anyone with teenage children will know that some of the best conversations happen in the car, partly because people often open up more when they aren't being stared at. The fact that we can now look at each other during every meeting doesn't mean that we should, not least because 'body language' has become 'face language'. I know some executives who dedicate a key part of every day to one-to-one calls. During lockdown, people may have had lots of human contact but they still missed human connection. The two things are very different. During a one-to-one, your communication will often change markedly. Individuals might be more open, more vulnerable or even more challenging.

Finally, the words we choose really matter. If you ask a person – and especially an English person – 'How are you doing?', you will often get a pretty standard and rather unhelpful answer: 'I'm fine, thank you.' However, if you ask that question with greater precision or empathy, you will often get a much richer response. 'How is your energy?', 'How are you feeling?' or 'How's your mental health?'

The more we destigmatise the conversation about mental health in the workplace, the more people will open up and share. If individuals and teams can accept that 'it's OK not to be OK' and that they are not alone in feeling isolated or flat, we can start making some real progress. Step one in taking a proactive approach to your mental health is having the courage to talk about it. Dana Strong of Comcast talks powerfully about one of the benefits of remote working in a business environment: 'I've been told by a few sources that one of the positive impacts of Covid-19 and remote working has been the "humanising" of their leaders,' she says. 'Your colleagues see you getting interrupted by your kids, they see the inside of your home. The act of inviting people into your home via Zoom has created a greater sense of empathy.'

We are all learning new communication skills as we lean further into remote working. The playbook on exactly what these skills look like is yet to be written, but we do know that the simplicity of your content and the authenticity and candour of your delivery is as important as ever.

THE MOST POWERFUL COMMUNICATION GOES IN THROUGH THE HEART

The success of BBH during the 1980s and 1990s came from their iconic campaigns for brands like Levi's, Audi, Boddingtons and Häagen-Dazs. Executive creative director and co-founder Sir John Hegarty perfected a form of advertising where rational information was communicated with huge amounts of emotion and style. At the heart of much of the agency's most celebrated work was a simple product point: Levi's jeans were 'double-stitched for extra strength'; Boddingtons beer was 'creamy'. But these proof points were elevated and amplified with such emotion that they became memorable. BBH shifted the language of the USP, the unique selling proposition, to the ESP, the emotional selling proposition. Hegarty knew that if you could connect emotionally with people, your message would be more likely to stick. 'Information goes in through the heart,' he would say.

Lawrence Dallaglio was always brilliant at engaging and leveraging emotion in a way that elevated performance when it mattered most. He makes the point that 'at the highest level, there is very little between the top teams tactically and technically – the difference can often be made in the head and in the heart. If you can connect there, it won't matter what is being said in the opposition changing room because they won't have a chance'. Maybe it was Lawrence Bruno Nero Dallaglio's Italian heritage that made him more comfortable with his emotions than the rest of us uptight English.

The Australian rugby legend John Eales is another fantastic communicator. He is one of the greatest rugby players ever to have played the game and also had the best nickname: 'Nobody', because 'Nobody's perfect'.

I was hosting a function in Melbourne the night before the second Lions Test in 2013, with the Lions one-nil up. An audience of about a hundred people had listened to Scott Quinnell and John talk about tactics and mindset, regaling the crowd with old stories that had them crying with laughter. As the evening drew to a close, I checked my watch and thought of the Australian team in their hotel, having their final meeting before a Test match that could see them lose the series. The meeting would have elements of fear and anxiety, and would need delicate handling by a captain. John was one of the best captains there had ever been. He'd won two World Cups, including one as captain, and a Lions series as captain. I put him on the spot and asked him what he would say to his team.

John was quiet for a moment, before saying he would ask the team to play for three groups of people. I won't be able to do his oratory justice, but it went something like this:

> I want you to play for the teammates sitting with you now. You know what you have all been through to get here tonight. I want you to play for the unknown fan. The Wallaby fan that follows you all over the world, who in all likelihood you will never meet, but who will follow this team to the ends of the earth. Lastly, I am going to ask you to do something. When you leave this room, I want you to pick up the phone or write a letter to the person who got you here. We all hold them dear, but we never tell them. I want you to tell them what it means to play for Australia and the role they have played in getting you here.

You could have heard a pin drop.

I arrived home about two weeks later. After some family time, I sat down and spent two days writing not one letter, but forty – to all the people who had helped me get where I am today but who I had never really thanked. Such was John's impact on me. No wonder we never beat teams led by him.

World-Class Communication: Highlights

1. Top teams over-communicate; dysfunctional ones don't communicate.

2. The leader sets the tone for communication, but they shouldn't be the filter through which all communication passes: there should be a web of interconnectivity between all members of the team.

3. What do comedians and presidential candidates have in common? They craft and refine their message with a real audience. Follow their lead.

4. Repetition is key. At the point that you're getting sick of the sound of your own message, it might finally be starting to stick.

5. Silence, body language, charts and pictures – words aren't the only tools at your disposal. Find what works for you, and don't be afraid to do it your way.

6. Do the hard work in advance, so you can be precise with your language but creative and instinctive with your expression.

7. Good communication goes in through the heart. If you can make your audience *feel* what you're saying, you've got them.

10. Teamship

*'Teamship demands that you question,
clash and speak up, irrespective of any
perceived hierarchy – whether you have just
one cap or a hundred.'*

DIFFERENCE TOGETHERNESS GROWTH

It is 7pm on 19 November 2003. In the England team room at the Manly Pacific Hotel, the starting team for the Rugby World Cup final has just been announced. Sir Clive and the coaches leave the room, and 22 names are listed on a flipchart for all to see. The problem, of course, is that there are 30 of us.

The starting midfield is Mike Tindall and me, which means Mike Catt has been left out. Catty had played a blinder off the bench against Wales in the quarter-final. He had been faultless against France in the semi-final, having replaced Tindall in the starting line-up. Now he was back to the bench for the grand finale.

What happened next will stick with me for ever. The players that took the initiative were those not picked in the starting fifteen. Mike Catt offered me a handshake: 'Well done, Shaggy. You know my mobile number and you know where my room is. Anything I can do for you in the next 72 hours so we can win this thing, just let me know . . .'

Much is written about leadership, but the skills of teamship are often under-explored and consequently less understood. As we noted in the generosity chapter, senior executives will often be part of two teams: the team they lead and the team their boss leads. I've observed that many people can get to a stage in their career where they put far more energy into being a good leader than into being a good teammate. Teamship is more nuanced than leadership in many ways, but no less important.

The skills of good teamship are hard to define because they are often intangible. Your support for a fellow teammate might be manifest when you offer some fresh eyes on an issue, a sympathetic ear or a shoulder to lean on. If the team has been set up correctly, you will be operating in different lanes, with connected but discreet responsibilities. So the skill is to offer support without judgement and assistance without taking over. This can often be more emotional than functional, and these horizontal and peer-to-peer relationships are less clearly defined than the ones we have with our bosses or direct reports. There is input without responsibility, which some people find challenging. Good teammates don't try to do your job for you, but they are there to support you if and when you need them.

As we explored in the chapter on culture, the culture and behaviours of any team will always be set by the leaders and the most senior teammates. I spoke to Simon Middleton, the coach of England women's rugby team, about star player Emily Scarratt. 'I think the first thing to say about her is that she is absolutely loved by everyone in the squad,' says Simon. 'The best of the best are sometimes seen as, and can be, selfish and precious people, but not Scaz. She's the most selfless person you could meet. She has time for anyone, regardless. She'll work with any player, no matter how young, old, experienced or inexperienced. She is massively positive, she always has a smile on her face and although she never rips the piss out of people, she doesn't mind having it taken out of her, which is a good thing because she gets more than anyone. The girls rip her to pieces for being so angelic and perfect, and as much as she blushes and rolls her eyes at them, she just cops it.'

Emily Scarratt is clearly the real deal: a world-class performer and a first-class teammate. The qualities that Simon describes embody the very essence of teamship, qualities that we will explore throughout this chapter: trust, generosity, selflessness and positivity. Teamship is at the very core of togetherness. It is the bond that you create peer to peer, the glue that binds a team together. Teamship involves challenge and support. It requires you to express your differences but also to align around a shared set of goals. Teamship requires generosity and selflessness. It asks you to get your head out of your own specific area of expertise, and to think about the broader issues facing the team. First and foremost, teamship requires trust.

THE FOUNDATION OF TEAMSHIP IS TRUST

A ndrew Strauss knows a thing or two about teamship. He was the captain who, with Andy Flower as coach, led the England cricket team to the number-one world Test ranking. His Ashes record reads 'played four, won three'. Strauss says, 'Trust is the foundation of any team environment. Without it, people are unwilling to show any weakness or vulnerability, and as such, your group is not a team that comes through for each other in challenging times, but is rather just an assembly of individuals.'

Trust is built within a team by knowing that you can lean on a teammate and they will give you their support, without agenda or any sense of debt. The power of a team is that members can take turns to set the pace. You can step forward when you are feeling strong, and your teammates can do the same. There is no better place to see this dynamic in action than in the velodrome during the team pursuit track cycling event, in which one team attempts to chase another down. No individual can lead for the full four kilometres, so riders take it in turns to lead, setting the pace and providing shelter for their teammates. Each rider will spend roughly one lap at the front of the chain before swinging up the bank of the track, allowing their teammates to pass underneath, and dropping back onto the wheel of the last rider. The best teams maintain a consistent top speed that no individual could maintain, and get over the finish line together faster than any of the individual riders could.

It's a fitting metaphor for how a high-performance team shares the load. Every rider knows their role and will lead for exactly the right amount of time to deliver optimum speed for the team. Stay at the front for too long and you will compromise your teammates and your time; hold some fuel back in the tank and you will be doing the same thing. Each rider has to trust each fellow team member completely. This trust is built on the Wattbike in an empty velodrome and in the gym – far away from the bright lights.

You will often hear elite performers talking about the fact that when under the most extreme pressure, they remind themselves to trust their training, their processes and their teammates. It's important to try to create an inner monologue that reminds you of who you are, how you got here and who you have around you.

Like any culture, trust is built slowly, through actions and deeds, but it can be lost very quickly. Think of the people you really trust; they usually exhibit a few key characteristics. They tell you the truth, even when it is uncomfortable to hear. They do what they say they are going to do and put the collective ahead of any personal agendas. You know that come what may, they will have your back. We should be just as demanding of each other when it comes to earning trust in the workplace.

An executive who finds empowering other people difficult is saying 'I don't trust you' and a boss who is constantly micromanaging is doing the same thing. These people will be dramatically limiting their potential for growth if they are unable to trust their team. An effective way of landing this message to a poor delegator is as follows: 'Keep working this way and there's only so far you can go. You need to start trusting your team, or you need to start changing it.'

Trust is technical as well as cultural. For example, trust is the key to every defensive system in a rugby team. The moment you start trying to cover for your teammate rather than marshalling your own man or your own channel, the system breaks down. You have to focus on your own job, safe in the knowledge that your teammate will do theirs.

This isn't always easy, which is why radical candour is such an important part of trust and a defining characteristic of high-performance teams. Teamship demands that you question, clash and speak up, irrespective of any perceived hierarchy – whether you have just one cap or a hundred. If your teammate is not preparing properly or is making the same mistake repeatedly, they need to be told. The team is only *ever* as strong as its weakest link.

In business, colleagues often find this level of peer-to-peer honesty difficult, preferring to feed back to the leader and asking them to deal with any problems. However, this only increases tensions, as it feels like the person is 'telling teacher'. The relationship between peers can resemble one of bickering siblings, where only the parent can arbitrate and resolve conflict. This is why it's so critical for teammates to learn how to give and receive feedback to each other, creating a safe space where peers feel that their ideas are being made better without feeling attacked or undermined. 'Going hard at the issue and soft on the person' and framing feedback in such a way that the individual understands it is being given to make the team and the business better are subjects we covered in the chapter on feedback, but they are worth repeating here.

'If you are giving or receiving challenging feedback, it isn't because I don't like you – it's because we are trying to help the team grow,' says New Zealand rugby legend Dan Carter. 'We became brutally honest about the way we gave each other feedback. It was understood that we were always growing the team.'

CREATE A TEAMSHIP CONTRACT

INVESTMENTS   **WITHDRAWALS**

We introduced the concept of the team code of conduct in the chapter on culture, and it's a contract that helps the team police the big stuff as well as the minutiae. The key point is that if not dealt with quickly, small things have a habit of becoming big things.

'One of our agreed team behaviours, as part of our value "we are one team", was that "we wear the same kit",' says Kate Richardson-Walsh, the Olympic hockey champion. 'This seems like such an obvious behaviour for a sports team, but after a good team discussion, we realised that we needed this in, for good reason. As we moved through Olympic cycles, we were fortunate enough to receive new training kit. In one cycle we got a nice white sweater, which was perfect for training when it was cold. Unfortunately, in the next cycle we got different jumpers, which some players found less ideal for training. One player in particular continued to wear the old comfy white jumper, even though we'd agreed not to. It's easy to think, "Does it matter?" or wonder, "Is this relevant?" But by one player going outside of the agreed group behaviours, they were putting themselves first and the team second. Trust could be questioned, and perhaps in some teammates' minds, even broken. If they were prepared to ignore that agreed behaviour, what about the other behaviours? By explaining how this small action was affecting others in the group and having a conversation about how our behaviours can both positively and negatively impact our teammates, we were able to get back on track together.'

Something as small as training kit can become a source of tension and snowball into something more significant if it isn't dealt with quickly. An issue in the workplace that is left to fester will grow and create negative energy. Kate's story is a brilliant example of a team dealing with an issue early, and a perfect illustration of one of the key principles in her team's code of conduct: 'We stamp out fires early.'

In the workplace, an example of this might be something as seemingly small as punctuality. If an individual is repeatedly five minutes late – never terrible, but never actually on time – it can begin to really irritate the rest of the team. 'Everyone else can get here on time – why's Jon's time so much more important than everyone else's?' If this kind of low-level issue isn't addressed and frustration is allowed to build, you can end up starting every meeting on the wrong footing because you've failed to deal with a simple act of petty disrespect. 'Jon, you need to understand that punctuality really matters to us. If you can consistently be five minutes late, you can consistently be on time. Please show your teammates the respect of getting to the right place at the right time.'

'Stamping out fires early' is such a big and helpful idea. A team that allows issues to fester will never be as powerful as one that addresses them before they gather momentum. We have all been in situations where we held our tongue and came to regret not speaking up.

A code of conduct is a form of contract, almost always written down, but there is often a bigger, unwritten commitment that teammates make with each other. Teamship is all about what you give and take. In a high-performance team, the individual clarifies what they are going to bring to the team and what they might need from it. Unless it's understood by everyone that you get to make investments and withdrawals, you will not be able to optimise the nurturing and supportive power of the team. A good teammate will bring positive energy to the group, but they will also, on occasion, need to lean on team members and signal that they might be struggling. They will do this safe in the knowledge that this support will be reciprocated when a fellow teammate needs it. Elite teams are good at signalling how they will turn up for each other.

CHECK IN AND CHECK OUT

CHECK IN

CHECK OUT

The All Blacks rugby player Richie Mo'unga talks powerfully about the simple protocol that begins every training session with his club side, the Crusaders: 'The first thing you do when you see a teammate is fist pump and lock eyes. It says that you are present and that you are fully engaged.'

High-performance teams check in with each other, taking a moment to see how everyone is doing before they begin the day or the task at hand. The people within these teams endeavour to bring positive energy to the group, but they are unafraid to share how they are feeling. It's not always easy to spot the signs of a teammate who is struggling; the truth, of course, is that it takes a courageous person to ask for help – it's a sign of strength, not weakness.

It's good to start your week or day with a high-speed check-in with your team. It only needs to take a couple of minutes and might, over time, even be replaced with a simple thumbs up or a traffic-light colour. Taking the time to talk about how each individual is 'turning up' is time well spent. Spending a moment to focus on 'us' before we focus on 'it' is a good ritual to bake into your regular catch-ups. It doesn't have to be time-consuming – it just needs to be candid.

Try to get into the habit of creating 'bookends' at the start and end of your meetings. Checking out is just as important as checking in. It should be a whistle-stop tour around the group, making sure that everyone is clear on the next steps and on where responsibility for them lies.

A high-performance team will be comfortable 'signalling' to each other what they are feeling as well as thinking. People may not always want to talk about their problems, but they might well want to flag them. For example, they might say: 'I've got some challenges at home at the moment. If I'm looking serious or anxious, it's not because of you.'

In Latin countries, mourners will wear black for a period of time – not just as a sign of respect, but to signal to those around them, 'I'm fragile, please be gentle with me.' This kind of signalling would be welcome in many workplaces. A colleague may not always want to talk about their issue, but they may well want you to know that they've got one.

LAUGHTER IS THE SOUND OF TEAMSHIP

We all love teammates who, no matter what the context, are capable of generating laughter. It might be their jokes, stories, impressions or even just a look – some people have funny bones. You could put Iain Balshaw in a Tibetan monastery and he'd have the monks falling about in no time. These people are invaluable in any team. They are happy to make themselves the focus of the humour, and they are self-deprecating and humble. Every team I played in had such characters. With the British and Irish Lions, it was Stephen Jones in 2005, Rob Henderson in 2001 and John Bentley and Doddie Weir in 1997. These guys burn bright in the memory because they have that most special of human skills: they make us feel good.

Were I to bump into them on the street today, nearly a quarter of a century later in some cases, a beaming grin would break out and I would be transported back to those special tours. These people had a wonderful ability to understand the mood of the team and to know what needed saying, often in the most tense and stressful of situations. On long tours away from home, these people were golden because they lightened the load.

There is a line, of course, and they stayed on the right side of it. The mickey was taken and daft statements were picked up on – nothing could get past them. But they'd shine the spotlight on you for a few moments and then move on. You'd be happy to be awarded the yellow jersey of buffoonery, because you knew it would lift the mood. It was never nasty; it added energy rather than took it away. It tightened the bonds within the group rather than creating division.

I've never been one to throw anyone under the bus, but I could just as easily list the players who stepped onto the wrong side of this line. In fact, sometimes they had no idea where the line was. On a few occasions, I saw cruelty, point-scoring and even some behaviours that constituted bullying, none of which has any place in any team. I don't buy the idea that 'sport is a tough environment, so anything goes'. It's often wrapped up as 'good-natured banter', of course, when a bully is called to task.

I've spoken to a number of teachers who work with teenagers, and they all hate the word 'banter', because it is so often used to legitimise cruelty. In a world where cyberbullying is a clear and present danger, 'banter' is often used by the perpetrator as a defence. Over time, most of us learn how to tell the difference between the teasing that's given with love and the comments that are intended to hurt; the strength of our relationship with the individual helps to determine where the line is.

Ben Kay assures me that I remained just on the right side of the line in the World Cup final in 2003, when he famously dropped the ball while trying to score in the first half – but as the words left my mouth, I wasn't at all sure. Matt Dawson's soft pass was right into Ben's breadbasket; all he had to do was catch it and fall over the line. Ben had amazing hands – he could field in the slips to Jofra Archer if he wanted to – and for those of us watching, it happened in slow motion. If he had another thousand goes at it, he would catch every one – but down went the ball.

Our team code of conduct told us to support each other in these moments. It was our responsibility to pick up a teammate when he was low and get him focused on the next job. I was from the same junior club as Ben and had played with him for years, for Leicester Tigers and England. I watched and I waited as one by one his teammates wandered over to him with comforting words. 'Next job, Benny.' 'Don't worry, mate – we'll score from this scrum.' 'Make your next tackle, Ben, and we'll be good.' On it went.

Ben enjoys his chat. He's got a razor-sharp wit, as you'd expect from a lad brought up on the Wirral. He gives it well – and thankfully, he can take it, too. I waited until all my teammates had done their job and then walked alongside him. 'You'll regret that for the rest of your fucking life,' I said with a smile. He smiled back.

In the workplace, it's a special type of leader who can demand the highest possible standards while making the working environment fun. I know no better example of this archetype than Sally Abbott, managing director of Weetabix, who has this to say:

I've always believed that people respect authenticity more than authority, and as a Scouser, humour is a fairly important part of my make-up kit. Work can be hard! Targets to hit, growth strategies to create, brilliant people to manage – all of this is tougher than ever. Humour is so important to relieve the pressure – it's a unifier, it's the valve that releases the steam and, when used well, it stops us from taking ourselves too seriously. That said, laugh at yourself before you laugh at others. We spend half of our waking hours at work – you've got to make sure you have a bit of fun while you're there!

In a code of conduct that Ben created with a senior team recently, the team wanted to commit to the following words as their final teamship principle: 'We take our work very seriously, but we do not take ourselves too seriously.' Amen to that.

NOTHING BEATS WINNING TOGETHER

Why do international golfers celebrate the Ryder Cup like no other win? Because they know that winning together always trumps winning on your own. An individual triumph brings its own sense of reward and fulfilment, but you can't share it with anyone. You'll win alone and will most probably celebrate alone. Where's the fun in that?

Jeff Dodds of Virgin Media once attended a small dinner with Usain Bolt and asked the great man which medal meant the most to him. Jeff was expecting him to say one of his world record-breaking performances from the 2008 Beijing Olympics or the even faster times he ran at the following year's World Championships in Berlin, but he actually talked about one of his relay medals.

'What he explained was that so many events for an elite athlete are focused on the individual,' says Jeff. 'He said that if he wins the Olympic 100 metres he celebrates on his own, but if he wins the relay medal he celebrates with three of his closest teammates. He explained that in Jamaica, they prioritise the relay. They don't just prepare for it after the individual events are over. They work so hard at it because they value team success so highly. When it matters most, often against the Americans, the Jamaican team triumphs over a group of exceptional individuals. I'm not sure if Usain knew how profound a point he was making. I've taken that with me, that team success will always be sweeter than any success we achieve on our own.'

Usain Bolt is one of the greatest individual sportsmen of all time, and yet his greatest joy was winning as a team. They say that if you want to go fast, go alone, and if you want to far, go together. I think Usain might have done both.

This story is a reminder that no matter how brilliant an individual is, we are, at our core, social and collaborative beings. We need that sense of tribe, that feeling of togetherness, and that involves sharing ourselves openly and honestly with our teammates. When I interviewed the Curry twins recently, I was offered an interesting definition of teamship. Ben Curry talked about Dylan Hartley's captaincy of England on the tour of Argentina in 2017, saying that Dylan 'not only pushed us to be the best players we could be, he also wanted us to be the best blokes we could be. By that he meant offering up our personalities and ourselves for the good of the team.' The All Blacks have a simple mantra that 'Better people make better All Blacks', and I think the same is true of leaders and teammates. If you are decent, open-minded and generous, then those traits will turn up in the workplace. The bullies and the boors are most probably the same outside work, and you have to believe that they will get found out in the end.

Teamship is not just about the things you do together; it's about the way you feel about each other and how you look out for each other. A strong team will build powerful and invisible bonds that will last long after a team has stopped working together. I'm often asked, 'How many of the World Cup final team of 2019 would get into the 2003 team?' My answer: 'Not one of them.' 'But the team of 2019 pulled off one of the greatest single victories by an England team in living memory,' comes the argument, and I agree with that. But when you were part of something so special, you must leave it as it was. It can't be enhanced. You realise over time that it wasn't so much about the winning; it was about the people – the coaches, the squad, the team. I have the utmost respect for the players of 2019, but they are not 'my lads'. I'm willing to bet that if you asked them the same question, not one of our team would get into theirs. And that's exactly how it should be.

World-Class Teamship: Highlights

1. Winning together will always trump winning on your own – just ask Usain Bolt.

2. Trust is a non-negotiable; it is the foundation of teamship. Without it, you won't get anywhere.

3. Trust demands honesty – both in delivering honest and constructive feedback, and in sharing any issues or problems you might be facing.

4. Deviation from an agreed code of conduct, no matter how minor it might seem, will undermine your sense of togetherness. Small things can quickly become big things.

5. Make regular check-ins a part of your daily routine. Signal how you are turning up.

6. Laughter is the sweet sound of teamship.

7. Teamship isn't just about the things you *do* together; it's the way you *feel* about each other.

PART III

ACCELERATING
GROWTH

11. Training

'You only really get better when you explore your boundaries in training. You have to let go of control, understanding that control limits you.'

DIFFERENCE   TOGETHERNESS   GROWTH

In the days and years since that special night in Sydney in 2003, I've had time to reflect on my journey from England under-18s reject to World Cup winner. It was anything but a straight trajectory. It was packed with huge highs, but also gigantic lows: self-doubt, injuries and a family tragedy. But underpinning everything that happened, good and bad, was a desire to make myself better, to grow every single day. And so, fittingly, the final section of this book is the solution to the equation that we posed in the introduction, that difference multiplied by togetherness will naturally create growth. In all of our interviews, we found the desire to grow as a player, as a leader and as a team wherever we found excellence.

Growth is an objective and an outcome, but it is also a mindset. It is the relentless pursuit of becoming better. Great leaders will grow their business and their people. They will try to lift as they climb, to make everything and everyone bigger and better. They will understand that with growth comes opportunity and confidence, but also challenge. Part of growth is regeneration – casting off the old so that you can create the new. Growth can be painful – it will require you to put yourself into new and uncomfortable situations – but it can also be thrilling. An athlete loves a personal best just as a CEO loves a business win, because these are tangible illustrations that progress is being made.

Learning and training are different things in practice, but they are connected. Great training refines core skills and introduces new ones. In business, the leader needs to create a culture where learning is a central part of the working week.

Ben worked for many years with the strategist Jim Carroll, one of advertising's finest thinkers, who now has a hugely successful blog that explores the future of brands, communication and growth. 'I increasingly believe that the leaders of the future will be more like gardeners than generals,' he writes. 'They will create the diversity, the energy and the space for growth to take place. They will prepare their people for all seasons and all weather, at first protecting them, but over time giving them the skills and the strength to stand on their own.'

Rather than describing a general in the field, commanding and controlling, Jim is describing a model of leadership where the leader creates the environment for growth. They create the framework and the ingredients, but then also the space for individuals to grow – growth requires energy and diversity, but it also requires time. There will be all types of weather; the leader will not always be able to protect the team, but will help them build the resilience needed to cope with the seasons.

A CEO will want to grow revenues and profit, but they will also want to build the reputation of the business, the reach of the brand and customer loyalty. While they will be willing to buy in talent when necessary, they will also know that there is a special kind of satisfaction derived from nurturing your own.

This brings us to the causal relationship between learning, training and growth. Athletes understand that purposeful practice is the route to growth, that expert coaching is required for the mind and body, and that rest and recovery are important parts of training.

Sir Clive Woodward said, 'Elite athletes train for 99 per cent of their time and compete for 1 per cent. In the workplace, it's usually the other way around.' It is worth pondering the difference that a small change to those ratios could make to the performance and growth of businesses.

The inconvenient truth, of course, is that not everybody in the workplace loves training and many people have been scarred by a bad experience. The presence of bean bags is often an early sign that you're in for trouble. There might be some ghastly warm-up exercise meant to relax everyone but that actually does the opposite. There might be an overenthusiastic trainer or the dreaded 'trust fall'. Worst of all, the training on leadership or growth can be led by a trainer who you suspect has never grown or led anything. I've experienced all of this – and I bear the scars to prove it.

The business leaders that I most admire seem to create a virtuous circle of growth: they focus on their own personal development, which cascades into the growth of their team and then into growth for their business. They role-model curiosity, showing their direct reports that no matter how senior they are, they can always improve. They create a culture that understands the strategic importance of learning and development. They explain that growth attracts top talent and funds innovation, but most of all that it builds your confidence and gives you choices.

Sometimes it will be a new strategy or product that will create a burst of growth for a team or business, but sometimes it will be an individual. Hiring certain people can have a catalytic effect on your culture; they make everyone else better, setting new standards and helping you to rewrite your whole growth strategy. My old teammate Jason Robinson was a great example of this.

Jason's first training session as an England rugby union player was an unforgettable experience. We were playing a full-contact practice game and his team threw an intercept pass to Iain Balshaw, who possessed the kind of electric pace that looks effortless: he had hip sway, balance, control and astonishing speed. If Balsh made a break, no one bothered following him, but Jason didn't conform to our way of thinking. He set off, his legs travelling at a million miles per hour, while 28 players and 10 coaches stood riveted. The gap didn't close for the first 30 metres, but then Iain made his error. He looked behind him, and he tightened up. Billy Whizz's eyes didn't shift from Balsh's legs and his arms pumped. He closed in, with 30 metres to go . . . Getting closer, with 20 to go . . . 10 . . . Got him.

The revelation for me was not how Jason played, but how he trained. He drained his body of everything in order to improve, and in doing so dragged us into the sports science era. He also approached the technical parts of the game with the same level of focus. When he arrived in rugby union, he couldn't kick the skin off a rice pudding; by the 2003 World Cup, his spiral kicking was lethal and he could hit a dustbin from 45 yards with a drop punt. Jason showed us that you can grow to become whatever you train to be. He lent on the coaches, but he also watched and worked with his fellow players.

Businesses often under-utilise the training resources that are available within their own organisation. One can mistakenly believe that training always needs to be provided externally, but there is a win-win when you put together high-quality internal training initiatives: both the recipient and the trainer grow. Training is poor when it's theoretical rather than practical, 'off-the-shelf' rather than bespoke, divergent rather than aligned to the strategic goals of the business. One of the reasons that Ben set up The Growth House was his frustration at the quality of training services that he could buy externally, and because he felt that what he was creating internally was superior.

The ancient Greek poet Archilochus wrote, 'We don't rise to the level of our expectations; we fall to the level of our training.' Athletes understand that to get better, they need to train. They know that mind and body need to be worked if excellence is going to be achieved. In the workplace, the strategic importance of training is often less well understood. The training budget is often one of the first to be cut, training programmes can be poorly attended and they can be less than inspiring. Too often, training sits lower down the CEO's list of priorities than it should, not least because when training is good it is relevant, energising and bespoke; it's tangible and outcome-oriented. Good training is an accelerator of growth and change, so let's examine what it looks like.

TRAIN, REVIEW, RECHARGE, REPEAT

I've trained with some impressive people during my rugby career. Neil Back trained like a professional long before he was one, and Martin Johnson was a complete lunatic on the rowing machine. I've found that there are two types of trainers. There are those who need to know the full session, so they can pace themselves accordingly and work towards a crescendo. These are the 'last set heroes', and I'm still occasionally that guy. And then there are those who go all-out on the first set and empty the tank.

In 1998, a young Jonny Wilkinson turned up. Jonny never needed to know what the session was – he was in his own space. He waited to be told which line to start on, and when the whistle went, he did the exercise as if it were the last one he would ever do. He would wait to hear how much rest he had, use the time to breathe and recover, and when the whistle went he would do it all again. It was extraordinary and it was also contagious: over time, it became the norm for everyone. No questions, no pacing yourself, just total commitment to each individual rep. There was internal competition without threat, and a shared understanding that if we all got fitter, we would all get better.

Great trainers also understand the paramount importance of rest and recovery. They know that more can sometimes mean less – whether that means time off or lighter sessions – giving the body time to rest and regenerate, before coming back stronger and fitter. These athletes simulate game-day intensity in their training. They prepare their bodies for competition by making their training incredibly competitive. You may sense some contradiction between emptying the tank in training and prioritising rest and recovery; the consistent philosophy, however, is one of purposeful focus. If these individuals are training, they are training with real quality; if they are resting, they are doing so with real intent. Too many of us train in the limbo land between the two extremes, neither stretching our boundaries nor properly committing to our rest.

After our Rugby World Cup loss to South Africa in 1999, the training regime shifted a gear. These gear shifts and periods of accelerated growth often followed a big setback. We came to the humbling realisation that the big three rugby nations, Australia, New Zealand and South Africa, would be challenged by our bursts of brilliance, but would wear us down over 80 minutes. We just weren't fit or strong enough.

During the early 2000s, the Church of Pain, the state-of-the-art gym underneath the West Stand at Twickenham, became my second home. The Wasps and Quins lads – the likes of Lawrence Dallaglio, Jason Leonard, Dan Luger and myself – would meet up with Dave 'Otis' Reddin, our fitness guru, at 6.30am, train hard and then head to club training. Dave was also given much more time within our England training camps at Pennyhill Park to do his thing. Our strength and conditioning work became a central part of our training and not just a painful add-on.

Some mornings we just got it done, but for the bulk of the time we had purpose and intent.

SOMETIMES YOU'VE GOT TO EMPTY THE TANK

Dave Alred is a perma-tanned, roll-neck-wearing maestro who has worked with the best in the world in many sports, including Jonny Wilkinson and Johnny Sexton in rugby, and Luke Donald and Francesco Molinari in golf. Helping people develop technical ability under pressure is his absolute sweet spot, and he's a joy to watch when working with talent, young or old. It was Dave who first opened my eyes to the opportunities for growth that lie in 'the ugly zone', and I'll use his words from his book *The Pressure Principle* to define it: 'The ugly zone is the place where you try and fail, try again and fail – and continue trying and failing. It's the area just beyond your present ability.'

The ugly zone is the place beyond your comfort zone. It's the area of 'purposeful practice' where meaningful change and growth occurs. Dave wants you to find the ugly zone in every component of your game: to understand your work-ons and navigate a path to improvement through training. For youngsters, the message might be 'to sacrifice distance today for better technique and ultimately more distance tomorrow'. For Dave, it's all about the technique and the process. 'If you focus on the outcome and its implications, rather than the process,' he says, 'it will directly interfere with your ability to perform effectively under pressure.'

Eddie Jones loves the ugly zone. A training session with the England rugby team is like watching a Formula One team operate on grand prix day. Players race around like cars at breakneck speeds; coaches are waiting in different areas like pitstop crews; the transition between the different elements of training is seamless. They rehydrate, they debrief, they go again. The clock is always ticking. Eddie is often in the thick of it, but there are drones overhead taking in every detail for review later that evening. They work on their skills under fatigue and create a Test match intensity. It is spectacular to watch.

Elite cultures find ways of simulating game-day intensity in training. They put players under such extreme pressure that those feelings not only become familiar, but in some cases competing can feel easier than training. Dame Tanni Grey-Thompson won eleven gold medals in four consecutive Paralympics between 1992 and 2004. She has this to say about her most brutal sessions of the four-year Olympic training cycle:

> The phrase we used in our training group before our toughest sessions was, 'It's a good day to die.' A 30-mile fartlek was absolutely brutal, but totally necessary to build your base to be able to go for gold. There was no escaping it. There was no point being comfortable in a training session – comfort doesn't make you better. But the toughest sessions

needed to be signalled. Our hardest week was usually week three in our four-week training schedule. In that week, we would have to sleep in the afternoons and sleep eight or nine hours at night just to get through it. You can't operate at that level of intensity every week. That's the difference between training hard and training smart.

You only really get better when you explore your boundaries in training. You have to let go of control, understanding that it limits you. In business, we are often reluctant to put ourselves in uncomfortable situations. Many of us like to be in control, well prepared, expert even. But it is often in moments of extreme discomfort that our growth is most accelerated. We all need to get more comfortable being uncomfortable.

DO JUST ENOUGH HOMEWORK ON THE COMPETITION

A friend of mine from the Royal Marines talked to me about the first time a bullet whistled past him, putting his men in a real life-or-death situation. 'The first time I was shot at was a big surprise,' he said. 'My reaction was not. My training kicked in as I went through the drills I'd rehearsed so many times. One, take cover. Two, radio for support. When shot at, as soon as you've taken cover, you get on the radio and simply say, "Contact. Wait out." This lets everyone know that you are in contact with the enemy – they stay off the air, so you can request the assistance you need. It is a key part of the drill. Three, form a rapid plan. Years of drilling this response in very realistic training situations kept myself and others alive.'

Under fire, my friend composed himself, controlled his breathing and took confidence and clarity from his training. It's a similar story in sport, where one often hears about some players seeming to have 'more time on the ball' than others. The greats have the ability to understand the mayhem going on around them and to create order from chaos. They rely on their technique and their process, calling upon the skills that have been honed during thousands of hours of practice. Their training has turned a skill into an instinct.

When you hear Martin Kaymer talking about his 2012 Ryder Cup-winning putt on the eighteenth hole in Medinah – the climax of a European comeback known now as 'the Miracle of Medinah' – you see how his preparation has powered his performance. He says that he knew he would hole the putt. He just knew it. You might say that winners get to write their own version of history, but when you see him waiting for his turn and then lining up the putt, it's clear that he has a sense of calm confidence at a moment that would have had 99 per cent of the population struggling to hold the club. This is a sportsman using his thousands of hours of purposeful practice to give him the confidence he needs at the moment that matters.

In the workplace, you are always trying to turn best practice into habits and rituals. For example, getting teams to check in and check out, emphasising that the project isn't complete until the case study has been written, or rooting every discussion in the perspective of the customer. These things won't happen on their own – they have to be drilled into people. They have to be championed by the leader and repeated again and again until they become part of the daily and weekly routine. Good practices become good habits if you keep repeating them.

There is always a balance to be struck between preparing what you are going to do and preparing for what your opponents might do, and this raises the question of how much energy or 'air time' a coach should give to their opposition. I think you should show your opponent just enough respect and no more. If you've done your homework, you don't need to worry about the competition.

Martin Johnson used to be brilliant at this. On the Monday, we would all be looking at the All Blacks team and video clips of previous matches, scratching our heads as to how we were going to beat them. An element of humility and doubt would linger in the room – intangible, but definitely present. Then, as the week developed, we would identify some weaknesses in them and start to build an attacking strategy.

By the end of the week, Martin Johnson's 'finger jab' would be out: he'd be telling us how we would win and that there was no chance they would beat us. His self-belief was contagious. It spread through the team and made us all feel more confident.

In business, I think this same balance needs to be struck. You need to be aware of your competitor's positioning, strategy and execution, but you shouldn't obsess about it. It is due diligence to know how they are trading, but you mustn't become overly reactive. The bulk of your energy needs to go on executing your strategy and being your best selves. Do that and the competition will be more worried about you than you will be about them.

TRAINING NEEDS TO BE FUN

Progressive educationalists have understood for some time that rote learning numbs the brain and dulls the senses. There are big shifts taking place in schools and universities around the world to encourage more critical and creative thinking.

Sport has followed suit – it had to. I cringe when I recall some of the coaching sessions I took part in at school. The lack of imagination was staggering. We would be manhandled to stand in a particular spot and watch as a coach showed us how to do a particular drill a hundred times. This would leave about 30 seconds for us to have one go each. What inevitably followed was a total lack of interest from the group, a big drop in energy and a team that was lost to that coach from day one.

We do so much training as professional athletes, that it has to be fun. Of course you have to do the grunt work, but there also needs to be time set aside for purposeful play. By that I mean problem-solving, allowing players to find answers for themselves and to co-create. Play is handing over the reins to the players and allowing them to experiment. From the Monday morning warm-up to 'the captain's run' before a Test, there should be elements of fun and play in every session that get the creative juices flowing and put a smile on people's faces.

Daley Thompson is one of the finest athletes of all time. He won gold in the decathlon at the Olympic Games in 1980 and 1984, and broke the world record four times. One could argue that the decathlon champion is the finest athlete at any Games – the range of skills needed to run, hurdle, jump and throw at the highest level is breath-taking. If you close your eyes and think of Daley, it's very likely that he's smiling. He seemed to find a way of performing at the highest level while making it look fun. He'd done all the work and could lighten the mood to keep himself calm.

When I asked Daley how he approached his training, he said, 'When any of us first play sport, we play because we love it and because of how it makes us feel. For me, that feeling was all about doing it my way and having fun while I did it. It would have been more like a prison sentence to spend 350 days a year, training five to seven hours a day, if there hadn't been a lot of fun involved.'

TRAIN FOR THE TEAM OR BUSINESS YOU WANT TO BE

As a percentage of total costs, most businesses still spend very little on training – in many cases less than 1 per cent. Many companies tend to be equally frugal with the time they dedicate to training. An elite sports team will train for 99 per cent of their time and compete for 1 per cent, as Sir Clive Woodward noted. In the workplace, the opposite is often true – a small shift in that ratio could deliver big returns for businesses, as could a more strategic and purposeful approach to training. People like Jason Robinson and Jonny Wilkinson tried to simulate Test match intensity in their training; not many training courses in the workplace do that.

Great training should obviously focus on helping you to perform better, but it should also help you to transform *faster*. It should help you to grow *and* to change. You need to train for the team or company that you want to be rather than the one that you are.

It's critical that the learning and development agenda in any organisation is as dynamic and fluid as the business it is serving. It's worth asking yourself how much of your training is helping to accelerate change as well as growth.

Organisations will often experience 'growing pains' as they transition from one phase to another, as old systems and capabilities are stretched. In nature, a crab must cast off the shell that has protected it during its first phase of life before it can progress to the next. During this process it is vulnerable, because it is changing and growing. In business, knowing when the time is right to cast off the structures and processes that are stifling growth is a great skill. Sometimes, of course, this will mean people. The veterans of the last conflict will not always be the best suited to fight the next one. I'm not sure there is a bigger question in business than knowing what to change and what to keep. During these moments of transition, your training has to be thought of as an additional lever of change, reinforcing new messages and building new capabilities.

It's a challenge to ensure that your training is always up to date and future-focused. Too often, it is 'off-the-shelf' and geared towards legacy behaviours that are based on outdated thinking. Former special forces operator Jason Fox spoke about how the SAS has a rigorous debriefing process in the Feedback chapter. This method of 'closing the feedback loop' also ensures your training is bespoke and always relevant.

Try to shake things up, because routine is the enemy. It's easy to do the same things over and over again, in the mistaken belief that you are making progress. If you can create training intensity and become familiar with the ugly zone, when 'game day' comes the pressure will feel strangely familiar.

A good leader will prioritise the learning and growth of their direct reports. They will focus on what they teach but also on how they teach it; they will help you to build on your strengths and ideas and, in the broader scheme of things, to build your career. A good leader will take pride in the career progression and development of their direct reports, viewing their role as one where teaching and coaching are every bit as important as setting the purpose and executing the strategy. They will ensure that the learning and development agenda is aligned to the commercial agenda of the business. They will translate the growth of their talent onto the balance sheet, and beyond. Leadership, learning and growth are absolutely inseparable; they power each other. If leaders embrace and champion a culture of learning and training, all things become possible. Getting better is a journey that has no end.

World-Class Training: Highlights

1. Create 'Test match intensity' in your training and get more comfortable with being uncomfortable.

2. Make training fun – without trust falls or bean bags.

3. Do your homework on your competition, but don't overdo it. Show them just enough respect – and no more.

4. Train for the team you want to be, not the team you are right now.

5. Your training should help make best practice a habit.

6. Real growth requires spending some time in the 'ugly zone', the place beyond your comfort zone.

7. Good training must be kept up to date and made to feel relentlessly fresh.

12. Pressure

'It takes pressure to make a diamond.'

DIFFERENCE   TOGETHERNESS   GROWTH

On his Test debut in 2012, the England cricketer Jonny Bairstow was nearly floored, both physically and mentally, by the West Indies fast bowler Kemar Roach. He was hit in his sternum by a red leather missile travelling at 90 miles an hour. It was a tough introduction to the requirements of Test cricket, but what Jonny did next is the measure of the man. He knew his technique had been exposed, so he went away and developed coping mechanisms for operating under this most extreme pressure.

He spent the next 18 months facing fast, short-pitched deliveries from the bowling machine and from his teammates, under the watchful eye of England batting coach Graham Gooch. A batsman facing any delivery has to establish the flight of the ball, know where it will bounce, decide what shot he is going to play, get in position and then execute the shot. With a ball travelling at 90 miles an hour over the 22 yards from the bowler's end to the batsman, that leaves him just 0.45 seconds to do all of this.

To start with, Bairstow got hit, a lot. But as he persisted with it, his training bore fruit and he got better. Much better. Today, he is one of the finest players in the game against the short ball. Jonny explained to me that his hard work started for two reasons: one, because it bloody hurt; and two, because if word had got around that he couldn't face the short stuff, it would have been 'chin music' for the rest of his career.

'You learn to deal with pressure by putting yourself in uncomfortable places and learning to deal with it,' Jonny says. 'You've got choices. You have a choice of whether or not you go into your shell, hide, tell yourself it's not for you, say I should have done better or I should have done that. Or you go, "How do I contribute?"'

We all admire people who can perform to the very highest level when it matters most. We can be seduced into believing that being able to deliver on the biggest days is a talent you are born with. The truth is that, like most things in life, it can be worked on and improved. We explored the benefits of training effectively in the previous chapter, and learning to cope with pressure should be regarded similarly: as a skill that can be trained. Some people have trained themselves to be able to use the effects of pressure to their advantage.

Jeremy Darroch is the former CEO of Sky and the company's current executive chairperson. He says, 'Dealing with pressure is all about controlling your emotions under stress rather than letting them control you. Once you can do that, these emotions can be harnessed. With that mastered you can actually feed off pressure and use it as a stimulus to your performance.'

So how do the cream of sport and business harness pressure to make it a useful ally instead of a foe to be conquered?

YOU CAN ONLY EMBRACE THE PRESSURE WHEN YOU KNOW YOU'VE DONE THE WORK

In downhill skiing, poor preparation can result in terrible injuries. Konrad Bartelski remains Britain's most successful downhiller: in 1981 he came within 0.11 seconds of winning a World Cup downhill title, at Val Gardena in Italy. He describes how his preparation helped him deal with the nerves of facing the world's most feared downhill:

When arriving in Kitzbühel, it is impossible to avoid taking in that last, almost-vertical view of the Hahnenkamm. That daunting sight immediately gets the pulse racing. It is as if you are being presented with an unsolvable equation: balancing your fear with your excitement. It's the ultimate test of man versus mountain. The key to solving the conundrum is to turn all your negative energy into a positive force, to give yourself a turbo-charged energy boost. The management of this tension comes from focusing on the key task of finding the fastest line down the mountain. That 'magical' line would play out in my head like a repeating two-minute film, again and again. Programming the brain through every carefully planned scenario. My established pre-race routine would be to work on the rhythm of my breathing. Then instinct takes control, and so long as there is total commitment, the rest will follow. The courage for speed comes in the planning and preparation.

Konrad had trained and prepared meticulously; his confidence came from knowing that he'd put in the hours and was ready to race. This is a factor that crops up again and again with elite sportspeople: the commitment to practice and preparation so that, come game time, the pressure can be embraced, safe in the knowledge that the hard work has been done.

As we discussed in the previous chapter, we know we should put more resources and time into training in the workplace. But it's not just the quantity that counts when it comes to preparing for high-pressure situations – it's the quality, too. Jonny Bairstow tried to recreate the intensity of a Test match in his training so that when he came to perform for real, the conditions would not feel unfamiliar.

It seems strange to me that executives are reluctant to rehearse and simulate real-time business challenges with their colleagues. Why would you not practise a big fee negotiation with someone who could help you to prepare? There are only so many questions – why not practise all of them? Why not role-play a difficult conversation that you know you need to land with precision, or buddy up with a colleague who is an expert in the area that you're preparing for? A learning leader acknowledges that curiosity needs to be coupled with practice and rehearsal. The biggest coping mechanism Ben and I use for pressure is meticulous preparation. Very few things are daunting if you've prepared properly and practised them a couple of times, except maybe the Hahnenkamm!

YOU NEED TO SEE YOUR TEAM PERFORM
IN ALL CONDITIONS

In business we often learn most about our direct reports when we see how they respond when things go wrong. Did they lean into the problem quickly, ask for help and take accountability? Did they learn and grow? These are positive responses to pressure and warrant support, encouragement and empathy. Or did they choose to ignore the warning signs, shirk personal accountability and create a narrative in which the issues were produced by external factors beyond their control?

If the leader has created a culture of fear where nobody is willing to admit responsibility when things go wrong, they shouldn't be surprised when blame, cover-up and denial become the most consistent responses to pressure. Jeff Dodds of Virgin Media has a wonderful three-beat message regarding what he expects from his team: 'I need my team to get the job done, but I also need them to get it done the right way and to keep getting it done as the pressure mounts.'

We can all look good when things are going well in the absence of pressure, fatigue or anxiety. The world is full of 'fair-weather sailors', but to be world class is to hold it together in the eye of the storm, when it matters most.

In sport and business, there are things that you can control and many that you can't, so make sure you understand your variables. Sport may have fewer than business, but the philosophy is

221

the same. Rugby, simplified, has three: the weather, the referee and injuries. No matter what combination of those variables comes together, you should have a response that is well orchestrated and rehearsed. In Sir Clive Woodward's England team, we called it 'removing luck'.

We would do this by scenario planning and contingency planning – playing out potential situations so that if and when they happened, we would know what to do. We even had plans in place if we were reduced to 11 men – highly unlikely in a 15-a-side sport. But in New Zealand in June 2003, these protocols were tested when we went down to 13 players. We found a way to win, even though Lawrence Dallaglio and Neil Back both spent ten minutes in the sin bin.

If the pressure is getting to you at work and you're lying awake at night worrying about a problem, you might consider getting your team together and scenario planning your response to potential challenges and mishaps. No problem is as daunting when you've talked it through and mapped out a range of responses. At the heart of scenario planning is 'optionality', weighing up the pros and cons of different responses. Your problem is never as scary once it's up on the whiteboard. Just articulating the issue out loud is the first step towards resolving it.

Ben is a big believer in Edward de Bono's 'thinking hats' exercises, beautifully simple tools to help you manage pressure. First, you metaphorically put on a yellow hat and define your short-, medium- and long-term goals. The list can be long; it's not an exercise in focus or distillation, but rather one where you are painting a vivid picture of what success looks like. Then you switch hats, metaphorically putting on the black one and getting your team to try to identify the things that could go wrong. It could be a competitor move, a consumer or legislative change, an internal team challenge or a macro-economic one. You're not being negative, you're simply identifying potential obstacles, barriers and bear traps, so that you're better equipped to deal with them should they happen.

One of the Royal Marines' most famous mantras focuses on the concept of 'dislocated expectations': they say that 'the only thing you can count on in a battle situation is that things will not go according to plan'. The marines train rigorously so that when things do go wrong, they have the muscle memory and cognitive experience to respond. They scenario plan, create optionality and control the controllables. One common source of stress for executives and teams is a list of strategic imperatives that's too long – the team will be fighting on too many fronts. A way of reducing the pressure you're putting on yourselves is to shorten your list and focus on fewer, bigger things. Jeremy Darroch of Sky says, 'Success in business is often more about what you don't do, rather than what you do. The key is to make strategic choices and then deploy capital really aggressively against that strategy. These things are related, of course – if you're not completely aligned around your strategy, you don't really commit in execution.'

TAKE CONFIDENCE FROM THE PEOPLE YOU HAVE AROUND YOU

WHO HAVE I GOT AROUND ME?

My dad never fails to remind me about one uncontrollable in which I was 'bloody lucky'. My time in an England shirt coincided with that of seven or eight of the best players and two or three of the best coaches ever to represent England.

I think I knew this at the time, but the further I get from my playing days, the surer I become. I would look around the changing room and see greatness in the form of special people who were prepared to do whatever it took to improve. Standards were set, then raised. The bar was set so high that you either filled the space or someone else did. This was a group that you did not want to let down. In business, they say that great talent attracts great talent. In our case, great talent made good talent great.

When you are surrounded by excellence and you chase constant improvement, the confidence builds and victories can become a self-fulfilling prophecy. This was the kind of confidence Warren Gatland was talking about when he famously said that his Wales team had 'forgotten how to lose'.

We had confidence but we also had humility, and that's a really powerful combination. No one embodied those two qualities more than our captain, Martin Johnson. We were never allowed to feel like we had the right to win, but we also knew that our opponents would have to bring their A game to beat us.

I would find myself on the pitch three minutes before the team warm-up started, sitting down with my back against the post. I knew that a minute later, Richard Hill, Lawrence Dallaglio and Neil Back would appear out of the tunnel, immaculate in their full tracksuits. As they ran out, they would turn away from me and trot slowly around the opposition in formation, eyes in front. It wasn't confrontational. They weren't trying to pick a fight. It was just a simple statement: *Look at us if you want to, don't look at us if you don't, but be aware that we're here, and we're here to play.* I knew at that moment that there was only one team I wanted to be on.

We knew we could lose, and on a couple of big occasions we did lose. But we knew it would take a special team to beat us. What starts to happen over time in an environment like this is that you grow a foot taller when you look around at your teammates, and you want to make bloody sure that you don't let the others down. That's positive pressure, created by people setting high personal standards.

When it comes to framing pressure positively, your language really matters. Just think how you feel when the boss says, 'I know you've got this.' They are saying, 'The stakes are high and we both know that this is important, but I believe in you and know you can get this done. I'll be here to support and help if you need me.'

You can harness this key technique for managing pressure by 'checking in with *yourself*'. Special forces veteran Jason Fox explains: 'I would give myself a proverbial slap around the face by talking through three questions: Who am I? What have I gone through to get here? And who have I got around me?' Jason is making sure that his inner voice is building his confidence and not diminishing it. He is reminding himself that he is a special forces soldier with years of training and combat experience, and with world-class operators at his side.

We can choose to make our inner voice reassuring and positive, to drown out the doubt and the anxiety. It's a technique that's worth trying the next time you feel your pulse start to race and your heart quicken. Just remind yourself of who you are, all that you have done and the armoury of skills and experiences that you've built over time. Take confidence from the preparation you've done and the teammates you have. Think about the muscle memory you have built, and maybe even the scar tissue of failure. Then lean into that buzz of adrenalin and harness that heightened state of energy that we all need to perform at our best.

SOMETIMES GROWTH IS UNCOMFORTABLE

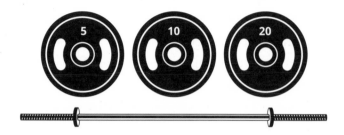

It's worth reminding yourself that growth requires pressure. You need to break a muscle down before you can build it up. Your periods of greatest discomfort are often your periods of greatest learning. A CEO recently told Ben that managing their business through the pandemic of 2020 and 2021 had been incredibly stressful, but massively rewarding from a learning perspective. They had learned more in that year as CEO than they had in the ten previous years. The great skill, of course, is to embrace the challenge and frame the pressure positively.

'I think we need to set our standards higher.' 'We have positive momentum, so how much better can we be?' These are the statements of teams and individuals who are putting positive pressure on each other and challenging each other's perceived boundaries.

The Olympic hockey champion Kate Richardson-Walsh tells a story about a gym session during one of her Olympic cycles. She was halfway through a session of weighted dips, when a junior teammate challenged her to put some more weight on the belt. Kate had a choice to make: should she get defensive and put the youngster back in her box, or should she embrace the challenge and load on some more weight? What's interesting about the story is that even Kate, who was captain at the time, and central to creating the team code of conduct, found it hard to accept the challenge the right way. She wasn't trying to coast, but the challenge was still hard to hear. She gathered herself, thought about the response she should be role-modelling and loaded on some more weight.

Great teams put positive pressure on each other on a daily basis, making performance their focus, safe in the knowledge that if they perform to their potential, the results will follow.

John Wooden was one of the greatest basketball coaches in history, winner of ten national college championships in a 12-year period with the UCLA Bruins. He wanted people to reframe the way they looked at their performance. 'Did I win? Did I lose? Those are the wrong questions. The correct question is: Did I make the best effort?' When that happens, he continued, 'you may be outscored, but you will never lose.'

If you respond to results rather than performance, you might change too much after a loss when you have performed well, and not enough after a win when you've performed poorly. Short-term wins can mask underlying problems, and short-term losses can hide the progress that you're making. That's why the performance, both individual and collective, is the metric that you should evaluate. When I coach, I like to make a distinction between errors of skill and errors of effort. I never mind the former – they happen. An error of effort, however, is unacceptable from a team or individual who is trying to get better. If you focus on the journey of getting better, short-term pressures become much more manageable.

It's a sentiment Denise Lewis agrees with. 'Looking back, it wasn't the end result I was most proud of,' she says. 'It was the process, the adaptation, the creation of a programme to suit a body that had limitations. We always knew there would be a better way of working, and we hunted them down, never settling. Working out how to be better became part of our way of life.'

Some individuals don't just cope with pressure – they actively thrive on it. One such athlete is Kevin Sinfield, the Leeds Rhinos and England rugby league legend. He faced plenty of pressure moments in captaining the Leeds Rhinos to three consecutive Super League championships, and learned to frame them positively. 'I loved pressure on the field,' he says. 'They were the moments that defined me as a player. Winning by 40 or 50 is great, but being 10–8 behind with ten minutes to go in a semi-final – this really excited me. This is when I had to earn my money. Being a kicker, those pressure moments were the reason I practised as much as I did.'

There are some people who don't seem to stand out during the course of everyday business, yet seem to grow in times of crisis. They thrive on the adrenalin and intensity of it all, getting better as the bullets start to fly. They are at their calmest in the eye of the storm – some of them even get a little bored and restless when things are going well. Many careers have been made by the way an individual chose to respond to a big setback.

FIND THE TOOLS AND TECHNIQUES
THAT WORK FOR YOU

When I interviewed the Olympic athletics legend Michael Johnson, I was struck by the way he talked about his pre-race process. He would isolate himself and create very high levels of alertness and focus, in stark contrast to Usain Bolt's approach. It seemed as if Bolt were just messing around and not taking things seriously, but Michael explained that his process was entirely purposeful: 'Usain knows that if he takes it too seriously, his nerves will drive him crazy. He knows what he has to do, and it works for him. What I did wouldn't work for him.'

In the chapter on communication, we discussed how each person has to find the way of communicating that suits them, and the same is true of coping with pressure. Every individual has to be allowed to manage pressure their own way. For some, that's sharing, for others it's going away to write and think – we're all different. What matters is that you are able to signal that you are feeling the pressure without any sense of shame or embarrassment. Over time, we learn to use that pressure to bring out our very best. An extrovert might want people around them on a rest day, while an introvert might want to be on their own. A strong team makes room for both approaches.

One's ability to manage the pressure on game day is directly related to the diligence and rigour of your preparation. Rio Ferdinand, formerly of Manchester United and England, has this to say:

My preparation was critical – it had a huge effect on how I coped with the big games. Knowing that I'd ticked all my boxes in the way I wanted, that I'd applied myself in training, been diligent with my mental preparation and done all the right things in terms of visualisation removed all the pressure that others may have felt about the same games. At Manchester United we were always involved in massive games, so it was important to make sure I didn't succumb to the pressure from the media – I didn't allow external events to impact, so I could be happy on match days. However big the match was, it was still just the same game I'd been playing all my life. I wanted to normalise my day on the big occasions, and my prep was key. I would have my coffee at a certain time and particular food. It was the same on normal days as on big days, so I could treat the big day like any other day.

Elite operators build their own processes for dealing with pressure, and while we might not be able to match the levels of the greats, we can all improve our performance when things get heated. A former colleague of mine who had served in the Royal Marines told me about the concept of 'combat breathing'. In a highly stressful combat operation, the optimal number of breaths per minute is a staggeringly low six – a three-to-four second inhalation and a six-to-eight second exhalation. Try it. After 60 seconds, you feel in control, calm and ready. So the next time you are starting to feel the pressure, why not give it a try?

The special players in sport understand that as the intensity of the occasion grows, so does the requirement to stay calm and in the moment. The brilliant Australian batsman Steve Smith calls it being 'in the bubble'. Play the ball, not the scoreboard; just make the next shot. In cricket, it's often the case that when one wicket falls, another soon follows, and the same thing happens in every sport: one error tends to lead to another. The mind gets jumbled and there is a discombobulation of the thought process under pressure. But the great players are able to reset and make a simple play. I find myself thinking of football players in these situations, the likes of Paul Scholes, Xavi, Kevin De Bruyne or Jan Mølby from the great Liverpool side of the 1980s – players who can put their foot on the ball and inject some calm into a frenetic match. Their approach fits with how I feel when the occasion gets particularly intense: do the next little thing right, because being successful is often about doing a lot of little things right consecutively.

There are people in the workplace who play a similar role, absorbing negative energy and protecting their teams. It is such a valuable skill in the pressure cooker of modern business. Like the proverbial swan, they glide on the water with no visible evidence of the effort taking place below the surface. They listen, reflect and then act. They slow down the tempo, make things look simple and exude a sense of calm purpose.

There are few situations that are more pressurised than an Olympic final, especially one that goes to penalties. Helen Richardson-Walsh won hockey gold at the 2016 Olympics, scoring one of her two penalties in the deciding penalty shoot-out in the final against the Netherlands. Her description of taking that penalty is a masterclass in how to create a positive inner monologue. Her positive mental process and complete focus on the technique rather than the result helped to ensure that she will go down in history as a nerveless winner who delivered under the greatest pressure and on the biggest stage. Helen recalls:

As soon as the final whistle went, I was making my thoughts positive. Inside, I was smiling and happy – I utilised self-talk to tell myself that I was glad it had gone to penalties. As always, my process had actually started the night before. In the Olympic Village, I said to myself, 'If we get a penalty, I want to take it.' I decided which side I would go – bottom left. There was a little extra thought process for the final, as I'd taken penalties against this goalkeeper before and I'd taken penalties in earlier rounds. I thought she would guess bottom left, but that's my favourite spot, so I decided I would still go there but commit to keeping the ball on the floor, rather than lifting it slightly. As soon as the umpire signalled for the penalty stroke, I stepped forward.

If you watch video footage of the match, you can see that Helen's body language is exuding confidence and authority:

> I was standing tall, putting my shoulders back, making eye contact. On the long walk to take it, it's easy for your mind to wander and be negative – if you start thinking about what's at stake, you can get yourself into trouble. On the walk, I chose to think about my technique and to remind myself, 'bottom left'. I said to myself 'tight core', 'tight right hand' and 'push through three balls instead of one'. On the walk up to the ball I actually got booed, which is really unusual in hockey and in the Olympics, but it actually helped me. It made me angry. The anger took away any nerves – for me, angry is good. I pushed the ball, with not as much power as I would have liked, but by keeping it on the floor it went in. It was perfect.

There is an assumption that elite athletes have no comprehension of fear or anxiety, that they live for the big day and 'eat pressure on toast'. But the reality is very different. Performing under pressure is what we live for, but that doesn't mean the anticipation doesn't eat away at us. The waiting can be truly awful.

I was a quivering wreck in the week before the World Cup final. I did not want to be the rugby equivalent of the South African cricketer Herschelle Gibbs, the player who 'dropped the World Cup'. The week was the longest of my life. I battled with a terrible secret: I wanted to be anywhere but where I was. I wanted to run away. I was ashamed of that thought. It felt cowardly. So it came as a strange kind of relief the night before the final to be sitting opposite Martin Johnson and watching him push spaghetti around his plate. 'Shaggy, why do we do this?' he asked. The pressure had even got to the great man. I wasn't alone and in a strange way it gave me some strength to know that he was feeling it, too.

World-Class Pressure: Highlights

1. Do your preparation properly and nothing will seem quite as scary – except maybe the Hahnenkamm.

2. Take confidence from the people you have around you.

3. Frame your inner monologue positively, so that pressure can become your friend for the big occasions.

4. Everybody handles pressure differently, but you can be sure that *everybody* feels its effects at times – even the great Martin Johnson.

5. Are you a Usain Bolt or a Michael Johnson? Experiment and find an approach to handling pressure that works for you.

6. If you focus on your performance, the results will follow.

7. Understand the things you can control and those you can't. There's no point worrying about the latter.

13. Setbacks

'Failure and growth are inextricably linked.
Pain is a powerful teacher.'

DIFFERENCE   TOGETHERNESS   GROWTH

The foot-and-mouth disease crisis of 2001 may seem like a strange place to start this chapter, but it was the reason that three of Ireland's Six Nations matches that year were postponed. They had been due to take place in the spring, but instead took place in September and October. We won our first four matches, but were left in the surreal position of having to wait six months for the Grand Slam decider against Ireland in Dublin. We had been playing some brilliant rugby and had scored 215 points in four games, but when the decider finally came round, on my 29th birthday, we lost.

Despite the result, we had still won the championship, so we had to collect the trophy in front of a wildly celebrating Irish crowd. It was humiliating, standing there listening to the 'banter' and having no choice but to take it on the chin. That feeling never leaves you. So you bottle it up, and you use it.

Between our loss to South Africa in the 1999 Rugby World Cup and the 2003 World Cup final, we had a very good win ratio – something like 90 per cent – yet I remember every one of our defeats, and they still hurt. But one thing is for certain: they all played their part in preparing us for the World Cup final in November 2003.

No sporting team or business can avoid setbacks or losses completely. Even a market-leading organisation will have days when it all goes wrong. What matters, of course, is how you respond in those moments, both as a team and as individuals.

Strong cultures will make sure that they learn and that they grow. Over time, they come to realise that however crushing these moments seem, they played an important part in the journey. Growth never comes easy, but these often painful experiences build scar tissue and muscle memory that are crucial for future success. Pain is a powerful teacher that burns learning deep into your memory. Setbacks provide context and contrast; when goals are finally achieved, your success tastes all the sweeter.

SUCCESS IS NOT FINAL AND FAILURE IS NOT FATAL

'As you get more senior, you learn to prepare the ground for a business to deal with setbacks,' says Dave Lewis of Tesco. 'They are devastating for the team that's involved, of course, but they are rarely fatal for the business. The impact of a failure is rarely as disastrous as people think or fear.'

Growth rarely happens in a straight line, and only with hindsight do you understand the contribution that losses have made to who and what you are. When I look back at my career, it's clear to me that the toughest period was the end of my time at Leicester, a two-year injury nightmare. Injuries are part of professional sport, but that doesn't make being injured any easier. A competitor, by definition, wants to compete, not sit on the sidelines waiting to heal, and despite my best efforts, I kept breaking down. There was my second shoulder reconstruction in 1998 (I ended up having five shoulder surgeries during my playing career). I'm not the most physical specimen on the planet at the best of times, and I found the mental part of returning to top-flight competition very hard. Trying to find the confidence to make big tackles against big men while one of my shoulders felt compromised was a real challenge, and I was racked with self-doubt when I returned to the pitch in the autumn of 1998.

Then, a mystery groin problem emerged in November of that year that would keep me out of action for eight months. Club blamed country for my injury, and vice versa. One of the big problems with a groin injury is that it is invisible. You don't need a sling or a crutch, and as you appear to be walking around OK, the whispers start to grow. Some people at Leicester insinuated that I was faking it to save myself for international duty. I was furious, and the memory of that accusation angers me to this day.

I flew to Munich in May 1999 to see Hans-Wilhelm Müller-Wohlfahrt, a doctor who is famous for treating injuries to sports stars such as Usain Bolt, and I was back on the pitch within four weeks. Sir Clive Woodward would pick me for the 1999 World Cup, despite the fact that I'd missed so much club rugby.

In the quarter-final defeat to South Africa, I had my good shoulder mangled by their winger Pieter Rossouw, and then, when I returned to Leicester, I tweaked my hamstring in training. But I could hardly not play, after everything that had happened. A year of answering questions about when I would be back had been mentally exhausting. I'd almost recorded a note on a Dictaphone to play to people who asked me when I'd be back: 'I am fine. I am working hard. I hope to be back playing again soon.'

When I returned to Leicester in November 1999, my form slumped, my confidence was shot and my body was broken. It was a perfect storm. And just at the time that I needed my club and my teammates to support me, I felt isolated and alone. Worst of all, I felt judged. When an international player returns to their club injured, there's always some frustration to deal with. You want to show your club-mates that you care every bit as much for club as you do for country, but I just couldn't stay fit or find form.

I had to admit defeat at Leicester and start again, but the lessons learned during those two tough years stayed with me. I learned that an injured player needs to be supported emotionally, as well as physically. I made a mental note to always reach out to teammates who were struggling with long-term injuries, especially ones that aren't visible. I can see in hindsight that I didn't perform for Leicester to the standard that I would have liked, but it was the damage done to my key relationships that made me decide to cut my losses and return to Harlequins. I needed a change of environment and a fresh start.

Nobody sets out to do a bad job or make a poor decision, but we all occasionally slip up. You learn over the years when the time is right to 'call it'. A bad situation is only going to get worse if you continue executing a strategy that isn't working. This can be really hard, especially if you are emotionally invested, but sometimes the context has changed and the market has moved. Sticking stubbornly to a plan that is no longer fit for purpose is the act of a leader who is not listening or learning. It takes courage and confidence to acknowledge a mistake and change course, not least because you don't want to look indecisive, but you should try to take some comfort from what you've learned. You should take accountability, of course, but you should also try to think of it as your plan failing and not you. It's an admirable form of resilience to acknowledge defeat without losing confidence. It's OK to take a moment to dust yourself down and absorb a painful setback, but there comes a time when you've got to move on.

When I spoke with the former England rugby head coach Stuart Lancaster recently, he talked about 'SUMO', which stands for 'shut up and move on'. Stuart had to face a very hostile media and public after England's World Cup exit in 2015. He was *persona non grata* at Twickenham, having failed to take England out of the pool stages in their home World Cup. After doing lots of good work with England prior to the tournament, he received vitriolic criticism following losses to Wales and Australia that resulted in a humiliating early exit. But what Stuart did next is a case study in resilience and recovery. He went away. He grieved. He listened. He learned. He studied other coaches in other sports, and then he came back to coaching at Leinster, playing a key role in the club's Champions Cup win in 2018. The Leinster players now talk about how Stuart is a better coach and leader for his experiences in 2015, not least because he knows that, despite being a very tough one, 'England 2015' was not his final chapter.

YOU CAN'T WIN BIG IF YOU'RE TERRIFIED OF LOSING

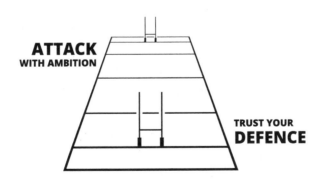

'A true winner knows how to handle losing,' says Alexis Nasard, CEO of Kantar. 'They know how to get back on the horse and go again. Setbacks happen – you have to train yourself to build the mental resilience and toughness to pick yourself up off the ground. It's not always easy. You might not have experienced too many setbacks, your fall might be very public, it might have hurt your pride, but winners get back on the horse and move on.'

Good organisations understand that failure and growth are inextricably linked, and that you can't really learn what works without understanding what doesn't. You can't avoid setbacks; the great skill is to mitigate the cost of them.

'Most organisations have processes in place that are designed to deliver a seven out of ten outcome,' says Andy Fennell, former CMO of Diageo. 'Processes de-risk, hierarchies de-risk. The best businesses, however, acknowledge that sometimes if you are aiming for a ten, you'll get a three. They don't reduce the risk of the three, but they do reduce the cost of the three. In Africa, we created a completely fresh approach to innovation, after years of failing to execute the global approach. We created mobile factories, with power and water attached. It was hugely successful, not because every idea succeeded, but because when we failed, it didn't cost us very much.'

There is a big difference between a team that is trying to win and a team that is trying not to lose. Defence is a massive part of elite sport, but if you cease to focus on attacking, you hand momentum to your opponents. A team that is trying harder to stop their opponents play rather than playing themselves becomes scared of the ball. We've all seen teams try to defend a lead and fail, when they should have kept playing. There will be mistakes when you attack with ambition, but if you trust your defence, that's OK.

ACKNOWLEDGE DEFEAT BUT
DON'T DWELL ON IT

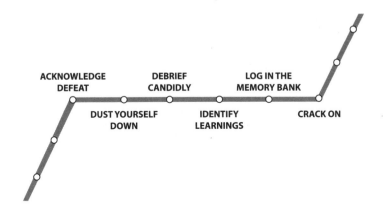

ACKNOWLEDGE   DEBRIEF   LOG IN THE
DEFEAT   CANDIDLY   MEMORY BANK

DUST YOURSELF   IDENTIFY   CRACK ON
DOWN   LEARNINGS

When I spoke to the SAS veteran Jason Fox for my podcast, I asked him how the special forces deal with setbacks. In the chapter on feedback, we described the after-action review, which is of particular relevance when something has gone wrong.

'The first thing you want to do after an operation is have a wash and go to bed, but you don't – you hit it while the iron is hot,' he said. 'You get everyone together. Someone guides the discussion and you go around the room, talking about what each individual did and why. It's not a witch hunt, it's just a grown-up way of looking at how you do things better next time. In the military, we acknowledge defeat but we don't dwell on it. You come back, you lick your wounds, then you bounce back and go again. Dwelling on that failure over and again puts you in a negative mindset. It's about using that failure, picking yourself up and making it a building block to being a better version of yourself.'

These immediate reviews can work just as well in sport and business. *The Test* is a brilliant TV series about the Australian cricket team that charts their course from the international disgrace of the ball-tampering scandal in South Africa in March 2018, to retaining the Ashes in England in 2019. I was struck by one particular episode, in which the Aussies have just endured a heartbreaking loss at Headingley, thanks to a brilliant century by Ben Stokes. To lose in such a manner is a bitter pill to swallow and the team is shell-shocked. After a sleepless night, the coach Justin Langer calls the whole squad together to watch every ball of Stokes's innings and analyse it. 'We're going to watch what happened yesterday, and we're going to learn,' he says.

At times, it is excruciating to watch – for the players and the viewer. Spin bowler Nathan Lyon can hardly bear it. But what is so impressive to me is that the team dealt with the loss immediately. They took it head-on, and this brutal review accelerated their healing process. A week later, they came back to win the fourth Test by 185 runs and retain the Ashes. It was a brilliant act of leadership – Langer led his players to a place they would not have gone to on their own.

Cultures that sweep failure under the carpet will continue to make the same mistakes, while cultures that accept failure as part of growth become bigger and better. Carolyn McCall, the CEO of ITV, views setbacks as a critical part of leadership development: 'There are always setbacks in every company, and in every career. It is always about how you approach them. They can be the most important thing in your learning. The more you are tested, the more you know about yourself – your resilience, your leadership, your motivation. So I always view setbacks, even when they make you feel awful at the time, as the most valuable development you can get as a CEO.'

So the key questions during a post-mortem have to be: 'What exactly went on out there?' and 'What did we learn?'

PAIN IS A POWERFUL TEACHER

RWC WIN

00 SCOTLAND LOSS	**02** FRANCE LOSS
99 WALES LOSS	**01** IRELAND LOSS

I've always believed that had England romped the Six Nations titles and won the Grand Slams in the build-up to 2003, we wouldn't have won the World Cup. The big setbacks kept us grounded and hungry. For four consecutive years, we lost one game in each Six Nations tournament, including the match against Ireland that denied us the Grand Slam. These are the painful lessons we learned:

Wales, 1999

England turned down the chance to put three points on the board with a kick when the team were six points clear. That would have taken England nine points clear and left Wales requiring two scores, but the lads went for the try and failed. Scott Gibbs then scored for Wales and Neil Jenkins converted. Game lost.

Lesson: Keep the scoreboard ticking over and get two scores clear.

Scotland, 2000

England went to Murrayfield with a plan to play an open, expansive game, but the match was played in appalling rain. Scotland played it simple and played the conditions. Game lost.

Lesson: Uncontrollables like the weather need to be factored in to planning.

Ireland, 2001

After the Lions tour to Australia, lots of our lads came back injured and Clive still picked us. We couldn't cope physically. Game lost.

Lesson: Don't pick anyone who is not 100 per cent fit. We would need 30 players to win the World Cup, not 15.

France, 2002

Our kicking game was too dependent on Jonny Wilkinson. The France flanker Serge Betsen got to him in Paris; he hounded and nullified him. Game lost.

Lesson: Build a broader kicking game beyond Jonny Wilkinson.

None of these lessons are hugely complex. In fact, they were all things we knew to be true beforehand. The difference is that when these theoretical principles become painful lessons, they are burned into your memory. A child doesn't need to touch a boiling pan twice to know not to do it again. Pain is a powerful teacher, and a scar is a reminder. All those lessons hurt like hell, but we bore the scars, we learned and we grew. In the 18 months after the

2002 defeat to France, for example, men like Mike Tindall and Jason Robinson, alongside the already brilliant Mike Catt, became world-class kickers under the tutelage of Dave Alred.

But these lessons aren't simply practical ones. There is a specific type of hurt that can build fierce resolve. Dan Carter talks powerfully about the infamous World Cup quarter-final defeat the All Blacks suffered against France in 2007: 'After the final whistle, we assembled in one of the bleakest dressing rooms of my career. We'd lost in the quarter-final of a tournament we were heavily favoured to win. It was only natural that there'd be anger and despair, manifesting itself in different ways throughout the squad. I retreated into myself, feeling blank incomprehension.'

A quarter-final loss is a national disgrace for the top rugby nations, and I was fascinated to see the following pattern emerge from the data:

1995: Australia go out in the quarter-final, then win the World Cup in 1999.

1999: England go out in quarter-final, then win in 2003.

2003: South Africa go out in the quarter-final, then win in 2007.

2007: New Zealand go out in the quarter-final, then win in 2011.

I know from first-hand experience that those quarter-final losses will have been very dark indeed, but the seeds of future success were planted in those desolate changing rooms. The fierce resolve was established – but the experience of those losses also forged some kind of special alchemy that bound the players together.

Maggie Alphonsi lost a World Cup final with the Red Roses at the hands of New Zealand in 2010, a narrow 13–10 defeat at a packed-out Twickenham Stoop. 'Through losing in a World Cup final, our team developed practical and tactical areas to improve on,' she says, 'but what actually had an impact was the emotional bond that was created between us. I truly believe an emotional bond is only created between players and staff when they go on a journey as big as a World Cup or Lions or Olympics, and you lose big together. We won the Rugby World Cup in 2014 [against Canada] because of the past losses that made us become more than a team. In that final, we went above and beyond for each other when it mattered.'

Ama Agbeze captained England to netball gold at the 2018 Commonwealth Games. She tells a similar story:

> We lost to New Zealand by one point in the semi-final of the Glasgow Commonwealth Games in 2014, and it had massive implications. It was absolutely crushing and took us months to get over. Our coach lost their job. The big lesson we learned was to focus on the moment and the process, not to worry about the outcome. Four years later on the Gold Coast, we used that pain and that learning to get the right side of the result. If you can be present in each moment rather than being desperate to be winners at the end, you'll often end up winning. We beat Jamaica by one point and Australia by one point to secure the gold.

Many business leaders will tell you that they learned the most during their toughest times. There is a very special kind of team spirit that is forged when your backs are against the wall. Leadership teams will often emerge stronger from a crisis, with relationships strengthened as a consequence of the shared experience. Thinking that is bold and creative will also emerge.

Just as some people function better under pressure, leadership teams often find that the bravest and boldest decisions are taken in moments of crisis. It seems counter-intuitive, but your thinking can be liberated when the environment changes dramatically. That diversification strategy you've been working on suddenly moves from being important to being urgent. While business success might make you complacent and put your innovation plans on the back-burner, there is nothing quite as emboldening as a sudden drop in revenue or profit to kick-start a winning idea.

WELLBEING AND RESILIENCE NEED TO POWER EACH OTHER

It is right and proper that we focus on wellbeing in the workplace and continue to destigmatise issues around mental health, and these are concepts that we will focus on in the next chapter. But wellbeing must always be coupled with an agenda that celebrates resilience and helps people cope with adversity. Care and empathy for colleagues needs to be coupled with grit and determination; kindness needs to co-exist alongside durability and positivity. Wellbeing can be thought of as the strategies that you put in place to nurture your own energy, while resilience is your set of tools for coping.

The agendas of wellbeing and resilience do not contradict each other; they power each other. The bigger your reserves of positivity and teamship, the more able you will be to cope in tough times. Of course, we all face negative thoughts, or times of crisis, when simply getting through the day is a good result. But on a more general,

249

day-to-day level, we each have responsibility for the energy and positivity that we bring to a group, and yet we often find it hard to call out individuals who constantly seem to sap energy. Some people might ask if it is acceptable to call out people who are consistently glass-half-empty in the workplace, but one elite culture is very clear on this topic. When Jason Fox explained the key pillars of the Royal Marines Commando code, one attribute leapt out: 'cheerfulness in the face of adversity'. I love that their code is actively saying that your energy and your contribution to the morale of your unit is not a 'nice-to-have', but a 'must-have'. In the workplace, we might think that some people are more naturally positive than others, but the marines are saying that we all have to do our bit. No matter how challenging the conditions or how negative your natural disposition is, you have to be cheerful to your colleagues. It's so simple and yet so powerful. The marines don't just ask for your positivity – they demand it.

In the life of any business or team, there will be good days and bad days, successes and failures. We must acknowledge that not only are they both part of the journey, but that they are subtly yet powerfully connected. If embraced correctly, a setback is just an accelerated and visceral piece of learning. It will equip you for times ahead and help you grow.

World-Class Setbacks: Highlights

1. Setbacks and times of crisis are an inevitable part of the journey to growth.

2. Failure is a learning opportunity, so use it wisely.

3. Defeat hurts, but it can build fierce resolve and sow the seeds of future success.

4. Failure is rarely fatal – the best teams bounce back.

5. The top organisations don't fear failure, but they do mitigate the cost of it.

6. Don't dwell on defeat. Once you've learned the lessons, you need to crack on.

7. 'Call it!' There comes a time when you have to cut your losses on something that isn't working.

14. Wellbeing

'You need to make sure that you look after yourself, because if you don't do that, you can't possibly look after anyone else.'

DIFFERENCE   TOGETHERNESS   GROWTH

S ir Clive Woodward did a brilliant job of building strong connections with all of his players. He created fierce loyalty and absolute followership. One of his secret weapons was his amazing wife, Lady Jayne Woodward. She always made sure that our wives and partners were included, and the match-day protocols for partners were completely transformed under her leadership.

As a big family man, Clive always understood the importance of family to his players. I experienced this first-hand at the start of the Rugby World Cup in 2003, when we were in Perth preparing for a critical group game with South Africa.

My wife Caro and I had lost our first child, Freddie, when he came prematurely into the world six months into the pregnancy in 2002. Rugby had allowed me to live again: it was my saviour, no question. A year after losing Freddie, Caro was pregnant again as I set off for the World Cup in Australia. We both desperately hoped that the pregnancy would progress without problems, but two weeks into the World Cup, the world came crashing down around us again. I received the call that I had dreaded from our doctor, Mark Johnson. 'It may be happening again,' he said.

I remember exactly where I was, standing in the stairwell outside the hotel's pool room. I went back in to put my cue down and excused myself, without saying anything to the lads. I turned first to my great friend Dave Reddin, our fitness guru, and then we went to Clive. I explained the situation that the doctor had laid out and suggested that I might need to head home. This was four days before the vital game against South Africa.

Clive was wonderful. Family first, no thought of the rugby. I was booked on every plane out of Perth and Clive said, 'If you need to go, we will understand and back you. There will always be a place for you to come back.' This moment was just one of the reasons why I would always go to war for Woody. I eventually decided to stay and play against the Springboks, knowing that Caro was in the very best hands. I scored and also made a complete howler, but that team meant everything to me.

We hadn't told anybody what was going on, and the second the game finished, Clive told the team in the changing room that I was heading home. I went straight to the airport and spent a week with Caro, after which she told me to head back to Australia. The deal we struck with each other was that she would keep the baby and I would go and win the World Cup. I travelled back, my head in a much better space, ready to fulfil my side of the bargain. It was a truly extraordinary piece of player welfare from Clive. He was, and is, world class.

In this chapter we will explore wellbeing, looking at energy, rest, mental health and resilience. A muscle can't get bigger and stronger if it isn't left to rest, just as a player can't focus on their training if their head is in a bad place.

Elite cultures understand that you can't possibly lead others if you aren't looking after yourself. They know that the quality of diet, sleep and training will directly impact performance. In the workplace, I'm often struck by how poorly people look after themselves, and then by how surprised they are when they feel tired, stressed or anxious.

Like everything in life, our wellbeing requires us to put in some effort – a set of behaviours that invest in and nurture our energy. It won't just happen if you don't pay attention to your sleep, hydration, diet and exercise regimes. Some have suggested that it should be called 'welldoing', so that people understand that it is an active pursuit that you need to make happen. The place to start is with self-care. Whether you're an NHS worker, a CEO or the captain of the local club side, you need to make sure that you look after yourself, because if you don't do that, you can't possibly look after anyone else.

PUT YOUR OWN OXYGEN MASK ON FIRST

'There were six hours to go before my team and I moved out of our base at the start of a very unpredictable operation,' my Royal Marine friend tells me. 'We had confirmed our plans and checked our equipment. I wanted to check again, but was confronted by my sergeant major. "Sir," he said, "I will do the checking. We will all depend on your decisions tomorrow, so make sure you get your head down." Over time, we called this mindset "proper selfishness" – making sure we are all in good enough shape to serve the people who depend on us has become a key principle for me ever since, as a leader and as a parent.'

This idea of 'proper selfishness' is intriguing. It means that before worrying about anyone else, you have to make sure that you are delivering yourself in the best shape possible to perform.

In a business environment, leaders can be prone to neglecting their own self-care. They can often feel pressured to be in the office first and to leave last – to role-model long hours and set an example for the troops. As a result, the leadership group, who are required to make strategic decisions and to think clearly and creatively, often arrive at work fatigued. They are in no fit state to lead and unable to pump energy and ideas into the business. The leader needs to accept that their energy and mental health are paramount – they need to be nurtured, protected and invested in. If getting home for the children's bathtime or going to the cinema recharges your batteries, then you need to be able to do that without feeling any shame or guilt.

A high-performance team will map out their year in a way that acknowledges when they will need to be at their absolute best. An elite athlete will plan their training in blocks, knowing that heavy work, lighter work and rest all have a role. Executives often fail to grasp this concept; they try to sprint through a 52-week year, failing to spot the inevitable gradual loss of energy and form. There are two interesting questions to ask your team: *when* exactly will we need to be at our best? And *what* do we need to do, before and after that period, to deliver sustained and long-term performance?

A modern leader needs to ask these questions and role-model a productive and impactful working day. If you are going to the gym at lunchtime, tell people. If you are practising mindfulness, *tell people*. Self-care is a critical part of world-class performance – you have to put your own oxygen mask on first.

PAINT A VIVID PICTURE OF THE FUTURE
YOU WANT TO CREATE

Dr Adam Carey is the founder of Corlife and is a doctor, nutritionist and leading commentator on all areas of sports nutrition and human performance. Adam was Head of Nutrition for England Rugby from 1999 to 2006, and has performed a similar role for the England Cricket team, the British Olympic Association, and a whole range of other elite teams. Through his company Corlife, Adam now runs health and wellbeing programmes for executives. There are two critical principles to his work. The first is visualisation, which is where he starts when working with an individual: 'If you can imagine where you want to be 20 years from now, you can paint an incredibly powerful picture; this vision then motivates you and allows you to hold yourself to account.' Ben was 49 when he started working with Adam in 2020, and one of the first things Adam asked him to do was imagine what kind of 70-year-old he wanted to be – the kind of father, husband and grandfather he envisaged. Ben painted a picture that's not unusual: an active life involving lots of sport, travel and the kind of activities with loved ones that would require him to be fit and healthy. The point that Adam then made was that if Ben wanted that lifestyle in his seventies, he needed to start making some sustainable changes now. Adam helped Ben to create a higher purpose for his wellbeing regime and connected his short- and long-term goals. As he says, 'Reviewing Ben's data, it was clear to both of us that there was a mismatch between his expectations and what his starting data was predicting – a mismatch that required an intervention and some significant weight loss. After losing 20 kilograms in nine months, Ben's expectations are much more realistic.'

This brings us to Adam's second key principle: the importance of creating incremental and sustainable change. Most dramatic changes and fad diets fail because the behaviours required are unsustainable. 'There is no better way to invest in yourself and your loved ones than by identifying easily achievable changes in your eating, sleeping and exercise habits that you can gradually improve over time,' Adam says. 'The small incremental steps to get there become manageable and no longer daunting.'

You need to give yourself a chance. Small changes that you can keep up for the long term are much better than big changes that won't last. I don't expect everyone to try to live like an Olympic athlete but with some small tweaks to your lifestyle, you can give yourself a chance of being the 70-year-old that you want to be.

CREATE A SPACE WHERE IT'S OK TO NOT BE OK

Companies like Headspace are proving that there is a significant global market for people who want to proactively invest in their mental health, and the business world is embracing this kind of activity at pace. At the time of writing, Headspace has 750 business clients, it has penetrated 20 per cent of the Fortune 50 companies in the US and Tesco has made the Headspace app available to its 400,000 employees.

We are beginning to address mental health in the workplace in a more meaningful way, but this is just the start. In the workplace, people still tend to be reluctant to share their vulnerabilities and anxieties. We might worry about being labelled and having it negatively affect our career progression. It's incumbent on us all to do a better job of removing the stigma around mental health.

Your team needs to know that we all have good days and bad days, and that signalling to each other when you're finding things tough is a high-performance behaviour. The reason that Ben encourages the teams that he works with to check in and check out is so that they can signal to each other what state they are turning up in. If the leader is willing to lower their guard and show some vulnerability, it makes it much easier for other people to do the same. It's a relief for many people to know that it's 'OK not to be OK'.

The archetype of the superhuman boss, with boundless energy, resilience and positivity, feels utterly outdated – not least because projecting an image of yourself as bulletproof and anxiety-free makes your team feel worse about their own anxieties.

In sport, we learned some years ago that you need coaches for the body and coaches for the head. 'Showing a vulnerable side doesn't come naturally to me,' says Helen Glover, the British rower who won Olympic gold in the coxless pairs with Heather Stanning at London 2012 and Rio 2016, and at the time of writing is going for gold again in Tokyo. 'On the rowing team, we had a sports psychologist and I would reach out to him and share my thoughts and emotions freely . . . before racing, I used to feel very negative and paranoid; sharing this with Robin helped me know that these were feelings I could use to my advantage.'

In the workplace, a good external coach can enable you to talk about things that you might find hard to talk about with your peers or boss. Trust has to be built, of course – rarely are we able to open up about our biggest vulnerabilities or concerns at the start of a relationship. But if the foundations of the relationship are laid correctly, a coach can help as a sounding board. Leadership can be lonely; a good coach can lighten the load.

Sharing vulnerability will always accelerate the growth of a team and the strength of the bonds within it. I spent ten years working alongside Scott Quinnell with disadvantaged young men for the TV programme *School of Hard Knocks*. We used the values of rugby to try to get young men from some of the poorest regions in the UK out of trouble and on to the jobs ladder. We had rough sleepers, ex-convicts, the habitually unemployed. At the start of every course, the lads were all poker faces and front – no one wanted to give anything away. But in every programme, there was a watershed moment when they dropped their façade, lost their bravado and showed their vulnerability. And once that happened, we knew we could start to build a team. It was an enormous mental obstacle that had to be overcome.

You don't need to build a raft or do a trust fall to learn about your colleagues; you just need to ask good questions, listen and learn. It's good for your wellbeing to really know your team-mates, but it's also good for theirs to know you. 'As soon as Heather and I learned to share our emotions with each other, it stepped up our competitive ability to a whole new level,' says Glover. 'The more you understand somebody, the more you know what makes them tick and the more you can get the best out of each other.'

In the 2005 British and Irish Lions squad, we had a week of preparation before we flew to New Zealand. We were paired up with players we didn't know and asked to find out about each other – to really find out what made one another tick. I found that the most revealing question was 'How do we get the best and worst out of you?' This knowledge is critical to the whole operation; it's as important as how you tackle and how you pass. You need to know the human being behind the athlete, to work out when to offer support and when to leave people alone.

Alex Danson was part of the gold medal-winning Great Britain hockey team at the Rio Olympics in 2016; by the time she retired, she had won 103 caps for Great Britain. When asked about the importance of sharing vulnerabilities and anxieties with teammates, she said, 'It allowed us to appreciate each other as individuals, respect that we are all different and what works for one wouldn't necessarily work for the other. It allowed us to see each other at our best and our worst and, fundamentally, we believed as a group this would make us stronger than any other team . . . and it did.'

BOOM

B.O.O.M.
BEST OUT OF ME

In a working environment, the exercise of sharing what will get the 'best out of me' – or BOOM – is just as effective an exercise as it is in sport. It is always fascinating to watch people who have worked together for years learning critical information about each other. An individual might hate confrontation, emails or even mornings. The act of sharing allows people to lower their guard and show their vulnerability, but also to educate their colleagues on how they want to engage. Figuring out how you like to work and what your expectations are of others shouldn't feel like a quiz, so give your colleagues a chance.

And just as a player in a sports team needs to know when a teammate could do with a helping hand, people in the workplace need to learn to spot the signs that a colleague is under pressure. Sometimes it will take someone else to tell you that you need a day off, a holiday, a gym session, a beer or to get out on your bike – just as it takes someone who knows what brings out your best and worst to understand when you're best off being left alone.

The act of telling your peers what brings out your best and worst takes some courage, but it always pays dividends. Not only do you build empathy and connection, you display where the areas of expertise are within the group. The leader should go first, to set the tone and demonstrate that it's a safe space. If they talk about the things that they are concerned about, it will legitimise others to do the same. They will open a door that often stays closed during normal day-to-day work.

The better your teammates know and understand you, the more likely it is they will treat you the way you want to be treated. Your mental health is best protected proactively – it's better to put a safety fence at the top of the cliff than a medical kit at the bottom. If people being late or rude causes you stress and anxiety, they need to know, in order to do something about it. If a Friday afternoon email will ruin your weekend, ask your colleagues to hold off until Monday.

As youngsters, many of us were encouraged to 'treat people the way you would like to be treated'; I am increasingly of the view that when it comes to leadership and teamship, we should treat people the way *they* would like to be treated.

IN EVERY LIFE THERE ARE SEASONS,
THERE IS SUNSHINE AND RAIN

Alan Jope, the CEO of Unilever, has a simple piece of advice for all his employees: 'When things are going well, there should be a little voice in your ear saying, "You're not that great." Likewise, when things go wrong you need that same voice in your ear telling you that you're not that bad. For your own wellbeing, you need to try to avoid the big highs and the big lows.' We've already observed that wellbeing and resilience need to power each other, with the former proactive and the latter more reactive. Alan is explaining that a more measured approach to success and failure will help you manage the ever-changing weather. Life is light and shade, sun and rain, yin and yang; these things don't balance each other or cancel each other out – they co-exist.

Victoria Milligan, the inspirational speaker who lost her husband Nick and daughter Emily in a horrendous boating accident, has learned a lot about resilience and wellbeing. The event left her feeling physically and emotionally broken, and 'terrified of her grief'.

During the early stages, Victoria was desperate for help, so she ordered book after book about grief and immersed herself in stories from other people who had been through life-changing situations. While most of them didn't help, one really resonated.

This story was of a young girl who had lost her nine-year-old brother when she was eleven. After the tragedy, the girl's mother was so consumed by grief that she withdrew from everyday life, leaving the young girl feeling like she had lost her mother as well as her brother.

It was a defining moment for Victoria. She thought to herself: *That will not happen to me or to my children. I have to find a way. To live and to find the joy of living.*

Victoria knows that she will always be grieving, but she also knows that she must focus on her own self-care if she is going to be the mother that she wants to be. She knows that she can't support and look after her children if she doesn't look after herself.

When you speak to people who have experienced extreme grief like Victoria, they will often say that they learn over time that grief, like happiness, is simply part of their new reality. They do learn to laugh again, but they still have very tough days. They learn that grief is as much a part of their life as happiness – like the seasons, they co-exist. Brian Bacon, the founder of Oxford Leadership, has a beautiful expression: 'In life, there is summer and winter. And winter passes.'

I know a little bit about grief. On 19 September 2002, my life changed. As I wrote at the beginning of this chapter, I am a father of four, but a parent to three. Freddie Greenwood was born too early to survive, but he lives with us still.

My mother-in-law Jane played an enormous role in helping us to live again. Family will always do that for you, but acts of extreme kindness from your inner circle never leave you, even after the difficult time has passed. My relationship with Ben was always strong, but certain things shifted the dial. Ben was the first person from outside of my family I rang that night from the payphone in the hospital. It was a Thursday night in London. Ben and his family were living in Singapore as his BBH journey gathered pace, which meant it was the early hours of the morning there. I couldn't speak for tears; my body had gone limp. We left the hospital the next day. Darkness surrounded us. Sleep was snatched in 20-minute bursts that Friday night, amid waves of inescapable, suffocating sadness. The doorbell rang on Saturday morning, and there, on my doorstep, was Ben. All work cancelled, with his family left behind in Singapore, he had come ready to listen, to say nothing – simply to be there for me. He later told me it was like looking at a ghost when I answered the door. It meant everything to me that he was there.

There were times afterwards when I thought life would never find any normality again. Yet from the grief came energy, the power to change, the ability to help. Freddie has a legacy: the mountains I've climbed, the countries I've crossed and the poles that I've reached have all been to raise money for premature birth research. I want to believe that Freddie's short life has made a difference. To myself, Caro and the many generous people who have supported us. Freddie made all those good things happen, and that makes me smile. I never thought I'd laugh again, but I have. You grieve for ever, but you learn to live with your grief.

Nobody leads a life without setbacks or loss. We all go through tough times – and we hopefully all enjoy some degree of happiness and success, too. We need to accept that both experiences co-exist, like the seasons they are just part of life. So be kind to yourself and try to be kind to all of those around you. You have no idea what battles they might be fighting.

World-Class Wellbeing: Highlights

1. Put your own oxygen mask on first. You can't look after anybody if you can't look after yourself.

2. For your own wellbeing you need to try to avoid the big highs and lows. You're never as good as people say, or as bad.

3. What brings out the best in you? And the worst? Make sure your teammates know.

4. A modern leader is comfortable sharing their vulnerabilities – they create a space where others can share their vulnerabilities, too.

5. A modern workplace should be a space where it's OK to not be OK sometimes. We all need to do more to remove the stigma around mental health.

6. Treat people the way *they* would like to be treated, not the way *you* would.

7. In life there is sunshine and rain – the tough times come with the good times, and it helps to accept that they co-exist.

15. Speed

'Elite teams can operate to the very highest standards, at the very highest speeds. In sport and in business, speed often wins.'

DIFFERENCE   **TOGETHERNESS** | **GROWTH** |

In 2002, we were training at the army garrison in Aldershot, where Harlequins were based for a couple of years. We were told that a leading sprint coach was coming to take the session: Margot Wells, a former international athlete who coached her husband Alan Wells to become the 1980 Olympic 100 metres champion.

We did some warming up, and then Margot told us what she had in store for us. Our session was going to be five 200-metre sprints, with five minutes' rest in between each one. A total of one kilometre on a lovely running track, on a nice warm day, with all that rest in between – we thought all our Christmases had come at once. There was one stipulation: each 200-metre sprint had to be run like it was an Olympic final. No problem, I thought.

However, I couldn't even finish the session. I just could not get up after the fourth sprint. When I finally did get to my feet, it was to be violently sick around the back of the old stand. I was in pieces. Eight of us started the session and only one finished – that was because he had been training with Margot for some time, and even he was on his knees by the end. The two-hour rest before the next training session saw seven of us in the changing room with the lights off and kit bags used as pillows, sleeping like babies. Our bodies had no idea what had just happened. Welcome to the world of the sprinter.

Straight-line foot speed can be lethal on the sports field. It offers a team the opportunity to attack space and stretch opponents. A defence doesn't have time to get organised, and players can't close gaps in the face of such pace. The average foot speed and top-end velocity of individual players are key performance indicators for all elite teams. The assumption is often that speed is something you are born with, but, like anything, it is something that can be worked on. Sprint coaches like Margot Wells will help the athlete get to higher top-end speeds when fresh and, crucially, when fatigued.

The fastest leaders and the fastest teams in any discipline often win – just read a bit of military history and you'll see this played out, time and again. Alexander the Great was quicker than his enemies, as was Napoleon. The blitzkrieg of the German Wehrmacht was an attacking system built on speed, and many of the greatest military innovations since the Second World War have been focused on increasing the speed of troops on the battlefield. It can cause your opponent terrible problems, because it's so hard to defend against.

Speed is an energiser and a differentiator. One of the characteristics of an elite team is that they can deliver very high quality at very high speeds. They will use communication to make everybody and everything faster. This might seem counter-intuitive, but they will also know that sometimes, the fastest way to win is to take a moment to slow things down in the short term, so that you are accelerating in the medium and long term. Everything in the book so far has been about giving you the tools for growth, and in this final chapter we will explore how delivering it all at speed, without sacrificing quality, offers an advantage. Speed, whether of body or mind, can be used as an accelerator for growth, so let's look at some teams and individuals who use it to devastating effect.

VISION IS NOT SEEING THE FUTURE, IT'S SEEING THE PRESENT FASTER

⇛FASTER

If you can see what is happening as it starts to happen, before anyone else, then you can put yourself where you need to be. Spotting an opportunity early and heading there is where mind and body meet. You might have the foot speed of Usain Bolt, but if you're running in the wrong direction, you will be late to the action. Making a calculated prediction as to where the ball is heading will allow you to get there faster. The great Canadian ice-hockey player Wayne Gretzky was taught by his father Walter to 'skate to where the puck is going to be, not where it has been'.

When looking for the next bright young thing to storm on to the rugby scene, I love watching players' movement when they don't have the ball. I observe how they position themselves in attack and defence. Sometimes a player will actually run ahead of the ball carrier, which seems to make no sense – you can't make a forward pass in rugby – but the clever player knows that they can slow down and let the ball carrier overtake them, thus allowing the movement to flow.

Vision is often described as the ability to see a future destination so vividly that you can navigate your way towards it. I like to think that it is less about crystal ball gazing and more about the ability to see the present very early – to spot an emergent trend early in its life cycle, to identify the start of a behavioural change, or to see a gap begin to open on a sports field or in a market.

In the same way that a gifted sportsperson might see space emerging or a defensive frailty before anyone else, a visionary business leader will quickly identify an emergent consumer change or a market opportunity. In this scenario, vision is about seeing just enough of something to give you the confidence to act at speed. Assessing data at high speed and making an early call is a great skill. We admire examples of 'quick thinking' and people who consistently make good decisions under pressure and at high tempo. They are often able to do this because they trust the instincts and skills that have been honed during many hours of practice and preparation. They can make confident decisions at speed because they've done the work. Time spent analysing your competitors' patterns and 'shows' will better enable you to recognise behaviours that emerge under fatigue or stress.

We talked earlier in the book about Colin Powell's 40–70 rule. An experienced athlete or business leader will trust their instincts and act as soon as an opportunity presents itself. This same truth applies to managing failure: 'calling it' early when something is not working is a speedy way of mitigating losses. To fail fast is much less costly than to fail slowly.

Some senior leaders can find this difficult. 'I would observe during my early career that senior people could often slow things down,' says Dave Lewis of Tesco. 'They could act as bottlenecks. I have always had the view that the leader should be a catalyst. You want to be an accelerator.'

Good leaders speed things up, removing obstacles and creating momentum. If you are going to speed things up, you need an understanding of all the key parts of your business, so that precious time is not wasted 'getting up to speed'. In the same way that a sportsperson's mastery of their core skills hones their instincts, a working knowledge of every element of the business hones the instincts of a CEO and accelerates their decision-making. You don't need to be an expert in every area, but you do need enough knowledge to ask the right questions and see the whole chess board.

Many iconic businesses are examples of a market disruptor finding a way to accelerate their systems and processes to enhance customer satisfaction. Just think how the consumer values things that are fast – phrases like 'fast food', 'fast-track' and 'same-day delivery' have all entered our vernacular. In sport and in business, speed often wins.

In a world that is spinning ever faster, the consumer appreciates businesses that can deliver their services at a high cadence. The Amazon founder Jeff Bezos is, at the time of writing, the world's richest person. He has always been obsessed with speed. The first Amazon recruitment ad, posted all the way back in 1994, read:

Well-capitalized start-up seeks extremely talented developers ... You must have experience designing and building large and complex (yet maintainable) systems, and you should be able to do so in about one-third the time that most competent people think possible.

Amazon is a business founded and built for speed. So ask yourself the question: what do we need to add to speed things up, but also, what do we need to take away?

INCREASING YOUR SPEED IS OFTEN DRIVEN BY WHAT YOU REMOVE, NOT WHAT YOU ADD

In big companies, it can often be the addition of unnecessary structure, process and stakeholders that add time. One senior executive in a big multinational once wearily said to me, 'We put a new organisational structure in place, but we leave the old one there, just in case.' The fastest way to speed up a process is often to remove layers of bureaucracy. You want your people focusing on quality creation rather than quality control. So if you want something done fast, build a small, empowered team and let them run.

In the workplace, I find that the simple mantra 'just enough' is helpful in resourcing tasks and teams. Just enough time, just enough budget, just enough resource. More people can often create more work; they can end up extending the timeline and increasing the budget, while leaner teams tend to be faster and more agile. Effective teams are often lean and mean. As Jeff Bezos famously said, 'If you can't feed a team with two pizzas, it's too large.' A small team will make decisions quicker, it will be able to change direction quicker and it will probably execute quicker, too. You need to resist the temptation to build big teams for important tasks. Some tasks need giant tankers, many need speed boats. A small, diverse and empowered team will be light on its feet. Ben worked with a TV producer at BBH who claimed that all she needed to do her job was an iPhone and a pair of Air Max trainers. Armed with the best of Apple and Nike, she could keep moving and keep things moving. When it comes to accelerating processes and increasing speed, less is definitely more.

GET SET EARLY

How you set yourself up and how you start really matters. I may go to my grave with this thought in my head. If you are ready to go on the 'B of the bang', there are exponential benefits for the team and the individual. Getting set early is a philosophy that can be applied to most things. You don't get a second chance to make a first impression, so how you start in a new job really matters, especially when you're in a leadership role. When he was promoted from his CEO role at BBH in Asia to MD of BBH's London office, Ben wanted to create a fast start for himself. He wanted to get set early, but he knew that the client and talent base had changed a good deal in the four years he had been away from the UK. So he put two significant initiatives in play.

The first was focused on talent. Three months before his return, he asked his new PA to create a document for him with the name, photo and job title of every one of BBH's 400 members of staff. He then spent 12 weeks memorising every name and face. When he arrived back in the UK in March 2006, he was armed with an amazing wealth of data. He began introducing himself to people and testing his memory: 'You must be Pippa. You work in finance, right?' It didn't take many successful introductions for word to get around that the incoming MD had taken the time to learn who all of his people were and what they did.

Step two was a client-focused initiative. Rather than starting in March 2006 with a host of internal inductions, Ben asked his PA to book 50 one-on-one senior client meetings. He spent the whole of March getting out to meet his new clients, taking a book, a pen and a load of questions. Through these 'client listening sessions', he achieved three things:

1. He made a big statement to his clients that his first task was to go and listen to his customers.
2. He made a big statement to his talent that he was very customer-centric and that he wanted BBH to be more customer-focused.
3. He very quickly got a 50-client perspective on the business he was running, which became a source of authority and confidence for 'the new guy'.

Both of these initiatives, one internal and the other external, manufactured a fast start for Ben. They allowed him to listen and to learn, but they also communicated a great deal about how he wanted to lead and what was important to him. Within a month of his return, he had laid some strong foundations that would allow him to accelerate his re-entry to the UK business.

How you start really matters. How you start in a new job, how you start your year, your day, your meeting. Human beings tend to sense and feel before they think, so the energy and the tone of any engagement is set in the first few moments of any encounter: are you on time, are you present, have you moved on from your last meeting? I always want leaders to think about their body language, their eye contact and their first few words. Get your start right and you're on your way; get it wrong and it's going to be an uphill struggle.

SLOWING DOWN TO SPEED UP

The very best know how to impose their tempo and technique on a game. They know when to increase the cadence and when to slow it down.

When I interviewed Michael Johnson, one of the greatest Olympians of all time, for my podcast, his breakdown of the perfect 200-metre sprint, delivered in his hypnotic Texan drawl, was spellbinding.

> You want to get up to race pace as quickly as possible. By 50 metres, I'm up to top speed . . . I might take three to four steps to relax, then get back at it. Coming off the curve, I'd be making decisions: Do I push? Do I continue with this pace? Then I come out of the bend and, like a slingshot, I'm coming down the straight. The focus then is just to minimise

any disruption to my technique. The smoother you are, the faster you will run. The more relaxed you are, the faster you will run. Resist the temptation to try harder – any attempt to do that will tighten you up and you'll slow down. You must keep balance and symmetry right to the finish.

Johnson's ability to slow himself down mentally and simply work on minimal disruption to his technique enabled him to maximise his speed, and he brought home the gold medal at the Atlanta Games in 1996 in spectacular style. 'The smoother you are, the faster you will run' is a beautifully simple expression from one of the greatest of all time.

Michael Holding, the West Indian fast bowling legend, is another 'GOAT'. As he says, 'Fluidity and smoothness adds to the efficiency of the delivery action, which naturally helps with increased pace and also contributes to longevity. And I stress "adds", because if you haven't got the natural ability to bowl fast, there's nothing to "add" to.'

Having the ability to slow ourselves down before we act is a critical skill. Inexperienced people often rush into action without taking a moment to reflect. Reviewing your options and pausing for thought will save time later down the line. The leading orthopaedic surgeon David Hartwright explained to me the key protocols when something goes wrong in theatre:

Surgery, however complex, is merely a series of steps or phases. Certain steps need greater precision, and consequently more concentration than others. Great surgeons recognise the importance of these phases; when you can relax into the operation, when you need to accelerate and when you need complete focus and accuracy. Unfortunately, the human body can throw you a curveball: unusual anatomy, difficult access, a divergent artery. Sometimes a phase is interrupted or complicated by one of these things and it can throw you off course. If, for example, there is a bleeding vessel and you're struggling to get control of the stage, the key is not to rush, not to get ahead of yourself, not to compound the situation with a wrong move. The key is to stop. Get control. If necessary, pack the wound, control the bleeding and go back to basics. Give yourself time to regroup, settle your nerves and get back on track. A domino effect of bad decisions is likely to end in a suboptimal result. And in surgery, that can be serious.

Jeremy Darroch of Sky explains how experienced leaders can leverage the time available to them: 'Make time your friend, not your enemy. There's always enough time – even under the greatest pressure, there's time to make good decisions. There are lots of things that we don't need to know or decide right now. When it comes to the moment, we will know, but right now we don't need to. So get comfortable with that uncertainty.' As he says, experience teaches you that you don't have to make all your decisions at once – taking the time to define which decisions need to be made will speed you up in the long term. 'The experienced leader is comfortable with uncertainty. I find that less experienced executives often search for certainty and clarity where none exists. With experience, you learn to stay in the process, you let the question repeat itself again and again, and then what tends to happen is that the answer comes to you.'

Any work that is done at such high speed that it needs to be redone constitutes wasted energy and time. Teams that use time well will map out a timeline and process that gives them just enough time upfront to assess their context. So take the first quarter of your meeting to review your context, asking if it has changed and if there are important new data points for review. When exploring your context or interrogating the problem, a great word to add is 'exactly'. What *exactly* is going on here? Why *exactly* is this happening? Who *exactly* is making this happen and how *exactly* does it impact us?

Too often in business, time is wasted when teams and individuals answer the wrong questions and are looking in the wrong direction. The environment might have changed, the business strategy might have evolved and a team can be left working on a project or problem that is no longer business-critical. Take a moment to ground yourself, and slow yourself down; in the long run it will speed you up, because a fast start can sometimes be a false start.

ELITE TEAMS CREATE QUALITY AT SPEED

I once spent a mesmerising ten minutes in a restaurant in Tokyo watching a team of top sushi chefs. It wasn't just their skill that was so awe-inspiring, it was the speed at which their skills were executed. Think of a great croupier or pianist; the convergence of speed and skill is often the most compelling thing. Elite practitioners and teams can operate to the very highest standards, at the highest speeds. They will bounce ideas off each other, provide different perspectives, interrogate thinking and reach a good decision quickly. They will use their purpose and their code of conduct to help guide their process. They will trust each other's instincts and respect each other's expertise. The absence of any one of these things will slow a team down, which is why the forming stage of a team is so important. Without laying the foundations regarding *what* the team stands for and *how* it's going to operate, you will start with a blank piece of paper every time you face a challenge. Protocols, processes and templates are all effective ways of codifying behaviour and speeding teams up.

The life cycle of a team is always worth monitoring, as individuals will need to go through a forming stage before they really hit their stride. The team will need to learn each other's strengths and weaknesses and build the relationships that allow them to challenge and feed back to each other with candour and confidence. A fast and effective team will have chemistry and shared experience, both of which require time and effort. But sometimes time is in short supply.

Bringing the team together quickly is the task facing every British and Irish Lions team in its first few weeks. Leaders like Sir Ian McGeechan are masterful at taking a group of individuals from four different nations and bringing them together. These are not the three-month tours of old, where team-building took place during months of provincial games and a more Corinthian approach to pre- and post-game bonding. The whole process is now accelerated, with the squad having days rather than weeks to define its identity, playing style and culture. But there are some things that still demand time and attention, and in the more recent tours it seems that there has been a greater appreciation for some of the more 'old-school' methods, albeit within an accelerated time frame. In 2017, there was a tour choir. It's reassuring to know that in the world of sports science and cryo chambers, there is still a role for team-building the old-fashioned way.

Most businesses will have a cultural leaning or norm. Some might enjoy the intellectual rigour of strategy so much that they tend to extend that phase of the process: 'Well, it seems to work well in practice, but how does it work in theory?' Sometimes the opposite will be true – a business might be so execution-orientated that the time set aside for strategy is consistently compressed. In either case, the leadership challenge will be to push against the norm, to speed up a culture that is prone to navel-gazing or slow down one that fails to review context.

This ability for high-quality creation at high speed becomes invaluable in times of crisis. 'During the Covid-19 crisis, we didn't need to create the intensity for change – we had it,' says Dave Lewis. 'That single-minded focus sped everything up. We knew that vulnerable people were isolating and that they needed to eat. When that became the pre-eminent goal, our team changed everything. Normally that would have involved decision-making that involved loads of people. Instead, we had six or seven experts, working remotely, and they changed the whole model in a matter of days. Remote working might even have helped rather than hindered. There is something about working remotely that allowed people to critically focus and prioritise. Our decision-making got sharper and faster.'

When I played for the Australian World Cup-winning coach Bob Dwyer at Leicester, he introduced me to the importance of responsiveness and the concept that there is no such thing as a bad decision. What mattered to Bob was how the collective reacted to each other's decisions. There was to be no throwing our hands up in the air or tutting loudly. He wanted us to continue to 'control the ball' no matter what, because if you did that, you had a multitude of options. If you focus on winning the battle in front of your face, then 'the opportunity is never gone'. The good teams react quickly; they respond at pace and stay alert and positive. They look after the ball and wait for another chance, which will often be just around the corner.

In business, there is nothing more energy-sapping than a long and drawn-out process. If you want something done, give someone a deadline. You'll often find that the most experienced people in an organisation are the fastest.

The great advertising creative Ewan Paterson, who created the famous 'Power is nothing without control' campaign for Pirelli, says, 'I'm not sure I got any better over the years, but I definitely got faster.'

Experience makes you quicker; it allows you to fill a toolbox with instruments and techniques that have served you well. Dave Lewis of Tesco shares this view: 'The question I've always asked myself is, "How do I put more tools in my kitbag, so that I can be a facilitator and an accelerator?" When I went to Argentina from the UK, it was because I wanted to find out if I knew marketing, or just one market. I like putting myself into places and opening myself up to skills I don't have. Suddenly I was in a different culture, with a different language and a different way of doing things.'

There are no short cuts to building this kind of wisdom or honing these skills. The concept of 'apprenticeship' is not very fashionable, because individuals are often in a rush for accelerated promotion when they should be focusing on accelerated learning. Focus on the speed of your learning, and promotion will surely follow.

The point we've made repeatedly in this book is that you can work on your instinctive decision-making, your responsiveness and your speed. A team willing to train will get better and it will get faster. The key accelerators will be trust, candour and cognitive diversity. An elite team will know how to stamp out fires early so that small things do not become big. They will see opportunities quickly, because they will be looking at the battle-field from different perspectives. And when it comes to execution, they will know what falls within their set of deliverables and what doesn't. A good team will know how to vary its speed; it will have gears, slowing down for a phase of strategic thinking and speeding up for a phase of impactful execution. Speed is hard to defend against and it is a differentiator, but most of all, speed is energising and exciting. In sport and in business, speed often wins.

World-Class Speed: Highlights

1. The very best teams create top quality at high speed.

2. Vision is not seeing the future – it's seeing the present, faster. Put the crystal ball away and look for emerging trends.

3. Speed is a competitive difference – think fast food, same-day delivery and instant decisions on financial services.

4. Take a breath – sometimes you need to slow yourself down in order to speed up.

5. Whether it's a new job, a new meeting or a new day, a fast start will get you out in front – but don't mistake a fast start for a false start.

6. 'Just enough' is a rule to live by. Leaner teams are faster teams. Just ask Jeff Bezos about his 'two-pizza rule'.

7. If you focus on accelerated learning, accelerated promotion will follow.

Conclusion

The changing room is all hustle and bustle, and there are hugs, photos, music, smiles, whoops and hollers. The World Cup winners' medals are draped around our necks and the laps of honour are complete, but 'We Are the Champions' can still be heard outside in the arena. Mike Tindall has sorted out the tunes in the confines of our 'shed'. Guests and celebs drop in, and there are more photos. I get a great one with Kyran Bracken and Iain Balshaw, all three of us connected to the school Stonyhurst College. Two of us are the sons of teachers at St Mary's Hall, the junior school. It makes me smile that the little Lancastrian village of Hurst Green was so well represented in Sydney.

Yet for all the energy of victory and the excitement of not knowing what the next 48 hours will bring, there is a strange reflective calm in the changing room. Maybe it is because we know that this side will never be together again, or maybe we are all still coming to terms with what has just happened.

Some people's bodies were in tatters. Jonny wouldn't play for England again for a long time. One of my abiding memories is the quantity of ice and strapping that was everywhere. We wanted to celebrate, but the 'self-care' protocols kicked in.

As the changing room emptied of guests, the last corks were popped and the hot showers began to work their magic. We were out of sync to begin with – everyone was doing different bits and pieces – but eventually we all found ourselves in our individual lockers getting changed. Oliver Sweeney shoes were laced and Hackett suits put on. The quality of our outfitting partners was just another example of the kind of detail that Clive had attended to. He had upgraded the quality of everything. Even our 'Number Ones', the post-match formal wear. Clive knew that when you wear world-class gear, you feel world class.

Then it was time to head out, but I'm not sure that anyone really wanted to leave the safety and isolation of the changing room. Deep down, we all knew that it was the end of a glorious chapter. Form, fitness and retirement meant this was this side's last hurrah. We knew that when we left the changing room, nothing would ever be the same – there were three new words that would be put at the end of all of our names for ever: World Cup winner.

In the time between that day and this, three other words have become central to how Ben and I have lived our lives, the belief system we've built and the message we try to share. It should come as no surprise that those three words are **difference, togetherness** and **growth.**

We focus a lot on the words we choose, but we also try to focus on how we make people feel. We hope that we've energised and maybe even inspired you. In life there are many things that are out of our control, it's reassuring to know that one thing we do get to control is how we make people feel. We are all players in multiple teams: with colleagues, friendship groups, siblings and partners. Our roles may be different, but good teamship looks and feels the same, whatever your role. Why not see how much positive energy you can pump into each of your teams?

Too often, the people we love the most get the energy that is 'left over'. Rather than seeing us at our very best, they see us when our energy is most depleted. So why not try to turn that around? Try thinking of your partner and family as 'Team One', and make the energy that you give them the first stone that you put in your jar.

We hope this book might accelerate your learning and growth – turbo-charging your career in the process. By taking the time to read and digest our ideas, we hope that you will become more purposeful, impactful and inspiring leaders. We hope that you will build teams that know how to challenge each other, teams that know how to give and receive quality feedback, teams that are brave and kind.

On that note, please send us your feedback, challenges and stories. We will continue to build this narrative, so your thoughts are critical to us. Please visit www.thegrowthhouse.co.uk and help us make this book better.

We also hope this might be a book that you revisit when you're starting a new job, building a new team or developing a new strategy. It's been a delight to put together, but it will only become real when human beings start responding to it. We want to know if we've prompted you to think differently, but most of all we want to hear if you've started to act differently.

But our greatest hope is that you will become evangelists for a new model of leadership and teamship. That you will role-model some of the 'world-class behaviours' that we've talked about. That you will learn but also teach, accelerating growth for your-self but also for the people that you lead and partner.

So please celebrate difference in all its forms and forge togetherness in all that you do. Do those things and you will grow well.

List of contributors

Sally Abbott
Ama Agbeze
Maggie Alphonsi
Brian Ashton
Brian Bacon
Jonny Bairstow
Konrad Bartelski
John Bartle
Sir Nigel Bogle
Sir Dave Brailsford
Jos Buttler
Dr Adam Carey
Jim Carroll
Dan Carter
James Cracknell
Ben Curry
Lawrence Dallaglio
Alex Danson
Jeremy Darroch
Jeff Dodds
Andy Fennell
Rio Ferdinand
Jason Fox

Nick Gill
Helen Glover
Tamsin Greenway
Dame Tanni Grey-Thompson
David Hartwright
Sir John Hegarty
Michael Holding
Wayne Hoyle
Philip Jansen
Michael Johnson
Alan Jope
Damian Lewis
Dave Lewis
Denise Lewis
Carolyn McCall
Karen Martin
Simon Middleton
Victoria Milligan
Richie Mo'unga
Alexis Nasard
Gary Neville
Tracey Neville
Paul O'Connell

Ewan Paterson

Rich Pierson

Matthew Pinsent

Helen Richardson-Walsh

Kate Richardson-Walsh

Scott Robertson

Jason Robinson

Emily Scarratt

Kevin Sinfield

Sir Andrew Strauss

Dana Strong

Geraint Thomas

Daley Thompson

Sarah Willingham

Sir Clive Woodward

Books

Dave Alred, *The Pressure Principle: Handle Stress, Harness Energy, and Perform When It Counts*

Po Bronson and Ashley Merryman, *Top Dog: The Science of Winning and Losing*

Ian Caldwell and Dustin Thomason, *The Rule of Four*

Ed Catmull, *Creativity, Inc.: Overcoming the Unseen Forces That Stand in the Way of True Inspiration*

Carol Dweck, *Mindset: The New Psychology of Success*

Malcolm Gladwell, *Outliers: The Story of Success*

Ben Hunt-Davis and Harriet Beveridge, *Will it Make the Boat Go Faster?: Olympic-winning Strategies for Everyday Success*

Acknowledgements

FROM WILL AND BEN

Thank you to Adam Sills at the *Telegraph* for commissioning our 'In sport as in life' series when live sport got shut down during the pandemic. Those eight articles were the genesis of this book and the catalyst for us getting started.

Thanks also to Lucy and Steve at Penguin Random House for being such wonderful collaborators and partners. The irony was never lost on us that when you're writing a book where receiving feedback is so central, you've got to be able to practice what you preach. We tried very hard to do that. We didn't always agree, but we did always respect your expertise and your craft skills. It's been a fantastic journey. Let's do this again some time.

ACKNOWLEDGEMENTS FROM WILL

The great John Eales inspired me to write 40 letters nearly 10 years ago to all the people who had played a part in my journey to Sydney in 2003. Coaches, medics, teachers, mentors, friends. I hope many will see their wise words and style of support in my writing. Thank you, again.

In my transition into the business world I have been offered so much help and been afforded so much time despite my commercial credentials being still in their 'start up' phase.

My wife, Caro, and daughter Matilda have allowed me to see life through a very different lens and have made me a kinder human being. I hope my writing reflects that.

To my boys, Archie and Rocco, If you're reading this, well done for getting this far!!

My Mum and Dad gave me my launchpad, picked me up when I was broken, and never deviated from total support without ever sugar coating anything.

My brother and sister are my own version of Ben Curry: loyal, trusted, fiercely proud and other than my ability to pass a daft shaped ball, are my superiors in all else.

Kalman, living out in Hong Kong, the best sounding board a friend could ever hope to have.

Finally Sir Clive, I'm not sure many others would have kept faith with a skinny bloke who didn't like contact much, and kept falling apart. Thank you for picking me for what I could do, rather than leaving me out for what I couldn't.

There are so many more I would like to thank, I will keep trying to learn something new from you all every day.

ACKNOWLEDGEMENTS FROM BEN

I want to thank all the clients, bosses, partners and direct reports I've ever worked with. I have learnt so much from so many of you. Top of that list is Sir Nigel Bogle. Nigel you are a master of your craft, an inspirational leader and a wonderful teacher. The relentless drive to make everything better is a trait that I think we identified in each other very early on in my time at BBH. Nigel I salute you.

Thanks to Brian Bacon, founder of Oxford Leadership. Brian

came into my life at the start of a big transition, and his coaching helped me to figure out what I wanted to do next and how I might do it. For that and plenty more I am hugely grateful.

I want to acknowledge all of the friends and family who have given me such high quality feedback, challenge and support throughout the writing process. Your 'fresh eyes' and candour have been invaluable. Thank you to my brilliant wife Amy, I continue to marvel at your brave and thoughtful leadership of our family. To my daughters Maya and Liv for your strength, love and encouragement. To my ever supportive Mum and Dad. To my dear friends Louisa and Adam, for looking at the big picture and the small detail, and to my brother down under Tobes, for constantly asking good questions. You have all been wonderful sounding boards. Whether it was on a zoom call, a bike ride, or over a drink, you have all made this book better. So thank you.

Finally to my son Joe. Joe your precision regarding our use of language and our articulation of the biggest ideas in this book has been genuinely world class. Thank you for making our narrative sharper, tighter and more precise. Your respect for words, and your commitment to using them accurately is a super strength. Your feedback was sometimes brutal, but always unswervingly honest. You have extraordinary things ahead of you Joe, keep pushing.

Index

Abbott, Sally 190
Agbeze, Ama 248
Ali, Muhammad 108
Alphonsi, Maggie 247–8
Alred, Dave 135, 205–6, 247
Amazon (online retailer) 10, 275
Andrew, Rob 141
Apple (technology company) 56, 142, 143, 277
Archilochus 202–3
Ashes 181, 244
Ashton, Brian 11, 130
Australia
   British and Irish Lions tour to (2001) 81–2, 188, 246
   British and Irish Lions tour to (2013) 174–5
Australia national rugby union team 30
   British and Irish Lions tour (2001) and 81–2
   British and Irish Lions tour (2013) and 174–5
   communication and 174–5
   culture of 139–40, 142–3, 204
   World Cup and 103, 241, 247, 284

Back, Neil 5, 15, 45, 155, 161, 203, 222, 224
Bacon, Brian 106, 266
Bain 31
Bairstow, Jonny 217–18, 220
Balshaw, Iain 5, 188, 201–2, 289

Barbarians 63, 96, 163
Bartelski, Konrad 219–20
Bartle Bogle Hegarty (BBH) xi–xii, 14
   Asia Pacific business xi, 54, 66, 146, 266, 278
   BBH London 54, 66, 277
   'black sheep' corporate identity 46
   bonus scheme 85
   Christmas company meetings and parties 148–9
   communication and 173–4
   culture and 144, 146–9
   decision-making and 66
   difference, celebrating/creative thinking, encouraging 46
   Dunk induction process 144
   ESP (emotional selling proposition) 174
   feedback and 27, 29
   generosity and 85, 90–1
   getting set early and 277–8
   innovation and 46, 50, 54
   management by mantra 126
   'power of difference to make a difference' 106–7
   purpose and 106–7
   selection and 14
   succession management 54
   Sunday Times 100 Best Companies to Work For list and xii
Bartle, John 106, 126
Bata 46

Bateman, Allan 90
Bentley, John 188
Betsen, Serge 94, 246
Bezos, Jeff 275, 276, 287
body language 151, 170, 172, 176,
    232, 279
Bogle, Sir Nigel 106, 107, 126,
    144, 156
Bolt, Usain 191–2, 194, 229, 234,
    239, 273
bonus schemes 84, 85, 153
BOOM ('best out of me') 263–4
Bracken, Kyran 289
Brady, Tom 135
Brailsford, Sir Dave 113–14, 121
brain trust 51–2
Branson, Richard 56
Brin, Sergey 148
British and Irish Lions 5, 166, 169
    communication and 174–5
    culture and 154–5
    decision-making and 71–2
    feedback and 29–30
    generosity and 81, 82, 88, 90
    high-quality creation at high
        speed 283
    selection and 19
    setbacks and 246
    teamship and 188
    tour to Australia (2001) 72, 81–2,
        188, 246
    tour to Australia (2013) 174–5
    tour to New Zealand (2005) 30,
        188, 263
    tour to New Zealand (2017) 283–4
    tour to South Africa (1997)
        29–30, 82, 90, 154–5, 188
    tour to South Africa (2009) 154–5
    wellbeing and 263
Brumbies 140
BT 12, 72
Buttler, Jos 147

Calder, Dr Sherylle (Eye Doctor) 38–9
Campese, David 139
Cantona, Eric 133
Carey, Dr Adam 259–60
Carroll, Jim 149, 200

Carter, Dan 37, 64–5, 109, 184, 247
Casa Nova 145
Catmull, Ed: Creativity, Inc. 51–2
Catt, Mike 82, 179, 247
Champions Cup (2018) 241
check in and check out 186–8, 194
Chicago Bulls 132–3
Christmas parties 148–9
Church of Pain (gym, West Stand,
    Twickenham) 204–5
Clooney, George ix
coaching xiii, 119–36
    decision-making and 73, 76
    defining 121–2
    feedback and 27, 32, 34, 35–6, 39
    freedom with responsibility,
        creating 130–2, 136
    impact of 127–30
    mantra, management by
        126–7, 136
    players and coaches, relationship
        between 122–3, 136
    positive 136
    psychological 127–30, 136
    selection and 5–6, 11, 12, 15
    special talent and 132–5, 136
    telescope (big picture) and
        microscope (next match, the
        next working day) 124–5, 136
    temperature, gauging and managing
        emotional and psychological
        128–9, 136
code of conduct
    coaching and 133
    culture and 150, 157
    feedback and 26
    pressure and 226
    selection and 19
    speed and 283
    teamship and 184, 185, 186, 190,
        191, 194
Cohen, Ben 5, 145
Commenee, Charles van 128–9
Commonwealth Games (2018)
    132, 248
communication 159–76
    crafting and refining message with
        real audience 169–71, 176

dialogue, controlling/staying on-
message 166–9, 176
heart, most powerful
communication goes in through
the 173–5, 176
high-performance teams over-
communicate 163–6, 176
leader sets tone for 176
mental health and 172–3
new world/new skills and 171–3
one-to-one calls 172
repetition and 168, 176
silence, body language, charts and
pictures 169–71, 176
words, choosing 172
Coode, Ed 55
Corlife 259
Covey, Stephen 150
Covid-19 19–20, 104, 147, 171,
173, 284
Cracknell, James 55, 91
Crusaders 63, 127, 186–7
culture xiii, xiv, 137–57
actions and words 149–51, 157
changing 152–4
code of conduct and 150, 157
cultures of ideas, elite cultures are
43, 46
dunking new people into 144, 157
fragility of 152–4
generosity and 83–5
international rugby national styles
139–41
on and off the pitch, strong cultures
built 145–9, 157
past, using 142–4
point of difference from
competitors 157
stories and 154–6, 157
tribe, sense of 154, 157
Curry, Ben 90, 96, 192
Curry, Tom 13, 17, 54, 90, 96, 192

Daley-Mclean, Katy 32
Dallaglio, Lawrence 5, 15, 123,
134, 161, 169–70, 174,
204, 222, 224
Daly, Elliot 52

Danson, Alex 13, 263
Darroch, Jeremy 218, 223, 281
Dawson, Matt 5, 161, 189
de Bono, Edward: 'thinking hats'
exercises 222
decision-making xiii, 25, 32, 61–78
bureaucracy, cutting/reducing
number of stakeholders 78
coaching and 123, 131
collective wisdom, harvesting
71–4
communication and 164
compass for, creating a 67–9, 78
core skills, mastering/trusting your
instincts 64–7
different perspectives/dissenting
voices and 78
fire in the belly and ice in the brain
76–7, 78
40–70 rule 70–1, 78
good player and a great player, key
difference between 63
people in the room who can make
things happen 74–6
purpose and 104, 111, 118
speed and 275, 284, 285
systems and protocols for,
building 64
Diageo xii, 8, 18, 48, 74–5, 242
difference, celebrating 1–97
decision-making and 61–78
feedback 23–41
generosity and 79–97
innovation and 43–60
selection and 3–21
Distill Ventures 48
Dodds, Jeff 12, 15–16, 151,
191–2, 221
Dragons' Den 16
Drucker, Peter 152
Dweck, Carol: Mindset: The New
Psychology of Success 36
Dwyer, Bob 54, 284–5

Eales, John 142–3, 174–5
easyJet 116
Edwards, Shaun 126–7
emptying the tank 205–7, 214

England cricket team 125, 147, 181, 217–18, 244, 259
England men's national rugby union team 143–4
  Argentina tour (2017) 192
  Clive Woodward and *see* Woodward, Clive
  coaching and 121, 122, 130–1, 134, 135
  culture and 143–4, 145–6, 155
  decision-making and 77
  Eddie Jones and *see* Jones, Eddie
  England Colts 27
  England Students under-21s 27
  feedback and 25–8, 38
  generosity and 88–90, 96
  Hannibal call 45–6
  innovation and 45, 47, 52, 57–8
  painful losses 245–7
    France (2002) 246
    Ireland (2001) 246
    Scotland (2000) 246
    Wales (1999) 245
    World Cup finals 247–8
  players *see individual player name*
  pressure and 222, 223–4, 228
  purpose and 103, 112, 117
  selection and 5, 13, 17–18
  setbacks and 239, 241, 245–7
  Six Nations 28, 38, 89, 108, 237, 245, 246–7
  Stuart Lancaster and *see* Lancaster, Stuart
  teamship and 179, 180, 192, 193
  training 199, 200–2, 204–5, 206, 212
  under-18s 25–6
  wellbeing and 255–6
  World Cup and *see* Rugby World Cup
England netball team 132, 248
England's women's national rugby union (Red Roses) 28, 32, 180, 247–8
ESP (emotional selling proposition) 174

face language 172
Farrell, Owen 141

feedback xiii, 23–41
  coaching and 121, 154, 163, 291
  communication and 163
  context and 26–8, 41
  culture and 154
  customer feedback forms 35
  daily habit of 41
  decision-making and 71
  feedback loop 30, 31–2, 213
  growth mindset and 35–8
  high cadence 31–4, 41
  innovation and 52
  'learn-it-all' rather than 'know-it-all' 41
  listening and learning, keep 36–40, 71
  negative 25–6
  setbacks and 243
  speedy response, requires 34–6
  teamship and 183–4, 194
  tough on the issue and soft on the person/challenging feedback delivered with kindness 29–31, 41, 154
  training and 213
Fennell, Andy 8, 18, 48, 242
Fennell, Ben xi–xii, 27, 28
  BBH, success at xi–xii, 54
  culture and 144, 146–7, 148–9, 150–1, 154
  de Bono's 'thinking hats' exercises and 222
  decision-making and 66, 69, 77
  feedback and 27, 28, 29
  generosity and 85, 90, 96
  innovation and 46, 50, 54
  pressure and 226
  purpose and 106, 107, 109, 111
  selection and 10, 12, 13–14
  speed and 277, 278
  The Growth House and xii, 150–1, 202
  wellbeing and 259–60, 261, 266–7
Ferdinand, Rio 229–30
Ferguson, Sir Alex 53, 73, 127, 128, 133–4
Flower, Andy 125, 181
Ford Coppola, Francis 69

Ford, George 52
Ford, Henry 59
Foster, Tim 91, 92
40-70 rule 70–1, 78
Fox, Jason 8, 30, 76, 88, 213, 225,
    243, 250
France national rugby union team 94,
    126, 140, 179, 246–7
Free State Cheetahs 30
Friends 167, 168
Froome, Chris 87, 114

Gatland, Warren 166–7, 224
General Electric 153
generosity xiii, 29, 33, 66, 79–97
    culture of, curation 83–5
    generous leader absorbs pressure
        and protects the team 93–4, 97
    player who makes every other
        player better (Richard Hill)
        88–91, 97
    purpose and 104
    rhythm setting and 91–3, 97
    Rob Henderson 81–3
    team name on the front of the shirt,
        your name on the back 86–8
    teamship and 181
    to yourself 95–6, 97
Genia, Will 142
Gibbs, Herschelle 232
Gibbs, Scott 245
Gill, Nick 13–14
Glover, Helen 261–2
Gooch, Graham 217
Google Mountain View campus 148
Great Britain women's hockey team
    13, 68, 184–5, 226–7,
    231–2, 263
Greenway, Tamsin 129
Greenwood, Caro 255, 256, 267
Greenwood, Freddie 255, 266, 267
Gregan, George 139, 142
Gretzky, Wayne 273
Grey-Thompson, Dame Tanni 206–7
Gröbler, Jürgen 121, 127–8
growth, accelerating 195–287
    pressure and 215–34
    setbacks and 235–51

speed and 269–87
training and 197–214
wellbeing and 253–68
Growth House, The xii, 150–1, 202
growth mindset 35–8, 46, 72, 75, 164
Guscott, Jeremy 140–1

Hanin, Yuri 77
Hannibal call 45–6
Harlequins 33–4, 240, 271
Harrison, Justin 82
Hartley, Dylan 192
Hartwright, David 280–1
Headspace 10, 16–17, 19, 57, 115,
    153, 260–1
Hegarty, Sir John 106, 126, 169,
    173, 174
Heineken 46
Henderson, Rob 81–3, 188
Henry, Sir Graham 71–2
Herbert, Daniel 82
Hill, Richard 5, 15, 82, 88–90, 97,
    145, 224
Holding, Michael 280
Horan, Tim 139
Howley, Rob 72
Hoyle, Wayne 67–8
Hunt-Davis, Ben: *Will It Make the
    Boat Go Faster?* 111, 131
Hunt, Natasha 'Mo' 32

'in the bubble' 230
innovation xiii, 43–60, 142, 201, 242,
    249, 272
    accelerator of growth, accelerator
        of change 47
    as art and science/blend of different
        skills and
        58–9, 60
    BBH and 46–7
    core skills and 49–50, 60
    courage and 55–6, 60
    force multiplier 56–8, 60
    fresh eyes accelerate 47–9, 60
    Hannibal call 45–6
    perfecting ideas/brain trust 51–2
    performing and transforming 49–50
    selection and 53–4, 60

Ireland national rugby union team
    151, 155, 237, 243, 246
Itoje, Maro 141
ITV 116, 151, 244

Jackson, Phil 132–3, 134
Jansen, Philip 12, 72
Jenkins, Neil 72, 245
Johnson, Mark 255
Johnson, Martin
  coaching and 134
  communication and 161
  culture and 141, 155
  decision-making and 77
  generosity and 93, 94
  innovation and 45, 46
  pressure and 224, 233, 234
  purpose and 112
  selection and 5
  training and 203, 209
Johnson, Michael 228–9, 279–80
Jones, Eddie 17–18, 52, 54, 73, 89,
    112, 168–9, 206
Jones, Stephen 188
Jope, Alan 105, 109, 114–15,
    168, 265
Jordan, Michael 133
'just enough' mantra 33, 276–7, 287

Kantar 46, 241
Kay, Ben 45, 46, 189–91
Kaymer, Martin 208
Keane, Roy 133
Kohli, Virat 135

Lancaster, Stuart 241
Langer, Justin 244
Larder, Phil 11, 35, 38
Larkham, Stephen 139
Last Dance, The 132–3
Lee, Brett ix
Leeds Rhinos 228
Leicester Tigers 190, 238–40, 284–5
Leigh, Joie 13
Leinster 241
Leonard, Jason 5, 145, 154–5,
    161, 204
Lewis, Damian 39–40

Lewis, Dave
  culture and 143, 150
  decision-making and 67, 69, 70
  feedback and 35, 39
  generosity and 84–5
  innovation and 50
  selection and 9, 19–20
  purpose and 104
  setbacks and 238
  speed and 274, 284, 285
Lewis, Denise 128–9, 227
Lincoln, Abraham 9
Luger, Dan 5, 204
Lynagh, Michael 139
Lyon, Nathan 244

Maidenhead RFC 35, 163
Manchester United 229–30
  Class of '92 53, 149–50
mantra, management by 126–7, 136
Martin, Karen 29
Martyn, Damien ix
May, Jonny 141
McCall, Carolyn 116, 151, 244
McCallin, Shona 13
McCaw, Richie 37
McElroy, Martin 131
McGeechan, Sir Ian 19, 154, 283
McKinsey 31
McLean, Lenny 161
'Me, We' 108–10, 118
Microsoft 38
Middleton, Simon 180
Miller, George Armitage 111
Milligan, Victoria 95, 265–6
Moody, Lewis 45, 145
Morita, Akio 59
Mortlock, Stirling x–xi, 38
Mo'unga, Richie 52, 63, 65, 186–7
Müller-Wohlfahrt, Hans-Wilhelm 239
Munster 151

Nadella, Satya 38
Nasard, Alexis 46–7, 241–2
Neville, Gary 53, 127, 128,
    134, 149
Neville, Tracey 132
New England Patriots 135

New Zealand
British and Irish Lions tour to
(2005) 30, 188, 263
British and Irish Lions tour to
(2017) 283–4
New Zealand men's national rugby
union team
coaching 139
culture and 141, 152
decision-making and 52, 63, 64–5,
71–2
feedback and 37
purpose and 103, 109
teamship and 184, 186–7, 192
training 204, 209
World Cup (2007) 247, 248
World Cup (2011) 71–2, 247
World Cup (2019) 17, 52, 168–9
New Zealand women's national rugby
union team 247–8

O'Connell, Paul 151, 154–5
O'Driscoll, Brian 72
O'Gara, Ronan 72
Olympic Games
(1980) 211, 271
(1984) 211
(1992) 91
(1996) 91, 280
(2000) 91, 111, 128, 131
(2004) 55–6
(2008) 113, 191, 261
(2012) 113, 261
(2016) 13, 68, 231–2, 261, 262
Owsley, Lily 13 134
Oxford Leadership 106, 266

Page, Larry 148
Paralympics 206
Paterson, Ewan 285
Pennyhill Park 134, 145, 205
Peppiatt, Jon 90
Pierson, Rich 10–11, 16–17, 19, 57,
115, 137, 153
Pinsent, Matthew 55–6, 91–2,
127, 128
Pixar 51–2, 143
Polman, Paul 105

Powell, Colin 70, 274
'power of difference to make a
difference' 106–7
pressure x, xiv, 20, 46, 215–34
conditions and 221–3
decision-making and 63, 64, 65,
76, 78
generosity and 93–4
growth, uncomfortable 226–8
harnessing 217–18
inner monologue, framing
231–2, 234
innovation and 46
people around you, taking
confidence from 223–5, 234
preparation and 219–20, 234
ubiquitous nature of 233, 234
setbacks and 248
speed and 274, 281
tools and techniques that work for
you, finding 228–3
wellbeing and 258, 264
'proper selfishness' 265–7, 268
Prozone 57–8
purpose xiii, 101–18
goals and 106–8, 118
'Me, We' and 108–10, 118
selection and 113–15
simple, sticky and realistic
110–12, 118
togetherness and 103–5
why before what and how 115–17

Queensland Reds 140
Quinnell, Scott 174, 262

Ramsay, Louise 146
Reddin, Dave 'Otis' 35,
204–5, 255
Redgrave, Sir Steve 91, 92, 128
Regan, Mark 146
remote working 32, 147, 156,
171–3, 284
resilience xiv
culture and 155
feedback and 36
innovation and 58, 60
purpose and 104, 109

resilience (cont'd)
  setbacks and 240, 241, 242, 244,
    249–50
  training and 200
  wellbeing and 256, 261, 265
Richards, Dean 141
Richardson-Walsh, Helen
  13, 231–2
Richardson-Walsh, Kate 13, 68,
  184–5, 226–7
Roach, Kemar 217
Robertson, Scott 'Razor' 127
Robinson, Andy 35
Robinson, Jason 72, 134–5, 141,
  201–2, 212, 247
Robson, James 82
Roff, Joe 82, 140
Rossouw, Pieter 239
Royal Marines 26, 207–8, 223,
  230, 250
rugby league 11, 126, 134, 228
Rugby World Cup, men's 142–3,
  174–5
  (1991) 54
  (1995) 247
  (1999) 204, 237, 239, 247
  (2003) ix, x–xi, 14–15, 38, 45–6,
    88–9, 94, 96, 103, 112, 179,
    189–90, 193, 199, 202,
    232–3, 237, 245, 247,
    255, 256, 289–90
  (2007) 247
  (2011) 71, 247
  (2015) 241
  (2019) 13, 17–18, 52, 168–9, 193
Rugby World Cup, women's 28
  (2010) 247–8
  (2014) 248
Rule of Four, The (Caldwell/
    Thomason) 25
Rumsfeld, Donald 48
Ryder Cup 191, 208

Sale Sharks 90, 134
SAS 8, 26, 88, 143, 213, 243
scale-up phase 16
Scarratt, Emily 28, 32, 180–1
School of Hard Knocks 262

Scotland national rugby union team 246
selection 3–21
  blend, magic is in 11–12
  customers and 12, 21
  difference drives performance
    18–20, 21
  difference, recruiting for 7–11, 21
  disagreements and 9–11, 21
  recruit in your own image, resist the
    impulse to 9, 21
  strengths and work-ons of the
    group 14–17, 21
  style of play, select for 17–18
  youth and experience, blend of
    13–14, 21
setbacks xiv, 235–51
  acknowledge defeat but don't dwell
    on it 243–4, 251
  communication and 164
  context and contrast, provide 238, 251
  fear of losing 241–2, 251
  innovation and 58
  pains as a powerful teacher 245–9
  purpose and 108
  Six Nations (2001) and 237
  success is not final, failure is not
    fatal 238–41, 251
  wellbeing and resilience and 249–50
Sexton, Johnny 205
Sinfield, Kevin 228
Six Nations 28, 38, 89, 108, 237,
  245, 246–7
Sky 218, 223, 281
Smith, Paul 57
Smith, Steve 230
Sony 59
South Africa
  Lions tour to (1997) 29–30, 82, 90,
    154–5, 188
  Lions tour to (2009) 154–5
South Africa national rugby union
    team 103
  culture of 140
  training and 204
  World Cup (1999) 237, 239
  World Cup (2003) 247, 255, 256
  World Cup (2007) 247
  World Cup (2019) 18

speed 269–87
  accelerated learning and 287
  competitive difference of 272, 287
  getting set early 277–9, 287
  'just enough' (driven by what you
    remove not what you add)
    276–7, 287
  quality at speed, elite teams create
    282–6, 287
  slowing down to speed up
    279–82, 287
  vision and 273–5, 287
St Mary's Hall 289
Stanning, Heather 261, 262
'start-up' phase 16, 130
Stirling, David 143
Stokes, Ben 244
Stonyhurst College 289
stories, culture and 154–6, 157
Strauss, Sir Andrew 125, 181
Stridgeon, Paul 167
Strong, Dana 6, 131, 173
succession planning 54
SUMO ('shut up and move on') 241
Sunday Times 100 Best Companies to
    Work For xii
Super 14 127
Super League 228
Surrey Storm 129
Sussex, Duke and Duchess of ix–x

'Team of Rivals' 9
teamship xiii–xiv, 12, 104,
    177–94, 290, 291
  check in check out 186–8, 194
  coaching and 133
  contract and 184–6, 194
  culture and 146, 150
  defining 179–81
  generosity and 83, 84, 85
  laughter and 188–91, 194
  purpose and 108
  resilience and 249
  trust and 181–4, 194
  wellbeing and 249, 264
  winning together, nothing beats
    191–3, 194
Team Sky 113

Tesco xii, 9, 19–20, 35, 50, 67, 69,
    70, 84, 104, 143, 150, 238,
    261, 274, 285
Test, The (TV series) 243–4
Thomas, Geraint 86–7
Thompson, Daley 211
Thompson, Steve 45, 46, 145
Tindall, Mike ix, x–xi, 14, 179,
    247, 289
togetherness, forging xiii, 99–194
  coaching and 119–36
  communication and 159–76
  culture and 137–57
  purpose and 101–18
  teamship and 177–94
*Top Dog: The Science of Winning and
    Losing* (Po Bronson/Ashley
    Merryman) 77
Tour de France 86–7, 113–14
training xiv, 197–214
  coaching and *see* coaching
  culture and 143, 145–6, 148, 151
  decision-making and 63, 65, 72
  emptying the tank/ugly zone
    205–7, 214
  feedback and 30, 32, 38–9
  fun and 210–11, 214
  habits and rituals and 207–9, 214
  homework on competition
    207–9, 214
  innovation and 49, 52
  pressure and 218, 220, 223,
    225, 229
  purpose and 111
  setbacks 239, 242
  speed and 271, 277, 285
  team or business you want to be,
    training for 211–13, 214
  teamship and 182, 184–5, 186–7
  'test match intensity' in 204, 214
  train, review, recharge, repeat 203–
    5, 214
  wellbeing and 256, 258
tribe, sense of 154, 157
Tuilagi, Manu 52

ugly zone 205–7, 213, 214
Underhill, Sam 13

Unilever xii, 39, 105, 114–15, 168, 265
US presidential election 167–8

Virgin Media xii, 12, 15, 151, 191, 221
Virgin Records 56
visualisation 229, 259–60
vulnerability, sharing 260–4, 268
Vunipola, Billy 141

Wales national rugby union team 103, 166–7, 179, 224, 241, 245
Wallace, Paul 155
Walters, Humphrey 47
Weetabix 190
Weir, Doddie 188
Welch, Jack 152–3
wellbeing xiv, 96, 253–68
  big highs and big lows, avoid 265, 268
  BOOM/sharing what will get the 'best out of me' 263–4
  incremental and sustainable change, creating 260
  mindfulness 10, 258
  planning/'proper selfishness' and 265–7, 268
  resilience and 249–50
  sunshine and rain, accepting 265–7, 268

visualisation and 259–60
vulnerability, sharing 260–3, 268
Woodward and 255–7
Wells, Alan 271
Wells, Margot 271, 272
Wilkinson, Jonny 5, 38, 58, 72, 94, 112, 135, 141, 145, 164, 203–4, 205, 212, 246
Williams, Steve 55
Willingham, Sarah 16, 58
Wooden, John 227
Woodward, Sir Clive 5–6, 11, 290
  coaching 121, 122, 130, 134, 135
  feedback and 26, 27, 38
  generosity and 89
  innovation and 47, 57–8
  pressure and 222
  purpose and 103, 112, 117
  setbacks and 239, 246
  teamship and 179
  training and 200–1, 212
  wellbeing and 255–6
Woodward, Lady Jayne 255
work-ons (things we could improve) xi
  feedback and 23, 33, 34, 35, 39, 41
  selection and 15
  training and 206

Zoom rule 32